This book is dedicated to my late father,
Charles David Gill who died in the summer of 2018
while Andy and I were writing this book. I sought his
advice on many of the devotionals you'll find here.

He was a real man of God and is the reason
I am the man I am today.

This is for you, dad. I love you and miss you greatly. - Bryan

HOW TO BE A MAN

LEARNING FROM
THE REAL MEN OF
THE BIBLE

ANDY BLANKS & DR. BRYAN GILL

FOREWORD BY RICK BURGESS

ARE YOU WILLING TO TAKE THE

HOW TO BE A MAN

CHALLENGE

We've crafted a pretty cool experience to go alongside this book. Now, you can do this book on its own and not miss a thing. But if you'd like to take your experience to the next level, we've created the "How To Be A Man Challenge." The challenge equips you to get the absolute most out of this book.

IF YOU'RE A DAD, THE CHALLENGE WILL HELP YOU AND YOUR SON GROW CLOSER TO CHRIST TOGETHER.

IF YOU ARE A GUY IN A SMALL GROUP WITH OTHER MEN, THE CHALLENGE WILL HELP YOU COLLECTIVELY BECOME THE MEN GOD IS CALLING YOU TO BE.

IF YOU'RE A YOUTH WORKER DISCIPLING TEENAGERS, THE CHALLENGE WILL HELP YOU LEAD THESE GUYS TO PURSUE CHRIST-CENTERED MASCULINITY.

AND IF YOU'RE JUST A MAN READING THIS BOOK ON YOUR OWN, THE CHALLENGE WILL GIVE YOU A WAY TO REFLECT ON WHAT YOU'RE LEARNING AND PUT IT INTO ACTION.

Sure, you can do this without taking the challenge. But don't you want to go bigger? Man up. Take the challenge.

GO TO HOWTOBEAMANCHALLENGE.COM

HOW TO BE A MAN: LEARNING FROM THE REAL MEN OF THE BIBLE

Published by Iron Hill Press, an imprint of youthministry360, Inc., in the United States of America.

ISBN 10: 1935832751
ISBN 13: 9781935832751

Executive Editor
Andy Blanks

Executive Producer
Rick Burgess

Art Director
Laurel-Dawn Latshaw

Copy Editor
Paige Townley

HOW TO BE A MAN

LEARNING FROM
THE REAL MEN OF
THE BIBLE

ANDY BLANKS & DR. BRYAN GILL

FOREWORD BY RICK BURGESS

TABLE OF CONTENTS

FOREWORD

When my schedule allows, I always look forward to having lunch with men that God has placed in my life to hold me accountable and challenge me. On this particular day, I was having lunch with a pastor friend of mine. We were in the middle of a relatively normal conversation when he looked me in the eye and said something I will never forget.

"Rick," he said, "if anyone else - a small group leader, a pastor, a youth pastor - is functioning as the spiritual leader for your wife and your children, then they are a better husband to your wife and a better father to your children than you are."

Wow. It hit me at that moment that the biggest threat to the church, the family, and our society are men who are ill-equipped to take on the God-given responsibility of being the spiritual leaders in these crucial areas of life. The problem was so obvious to me: there are men all around us who are not being discipled from spiritual infancy to spiritual maturity. It seemed so clear. But when I looked around, I didn't see much of a game plan in place to address this issue.

This conversation and many others around this same time began the journey that ultimately produced the first book in the "How To Be A Man" series. "How To Be A Man: Pursuing Christ-Centered Masculinity" challenged men to look at the one, flawless example of masculinity. The perfect example of true masculinity will always be when God decided to become one. And so the book called men to emulate Jesus Christ, the Son of God, the new Adam. The book continues to be consumed by men each week for the first time, and the stories we hear are powerful. But time flies, and all of a sudden, I turned around, and the first book was almost two years old. Men kept asking us, "When will there be another book"? Well, the book you hold in your hand answers that question.

Andy Blanks and the entire crew at Iron Hill Press have completely bought into the vision that God clearly showed us: if the church concentrates on discipling men as a top priority, then God will use those men to tackle the ills of the church, family, and society. And so it was such an honor when Iron Hill Press asked me to serve as executive producer to work with the team to produce more material designed by men for men. I humbly accepted, and this book is the next step in the "How To Be A Man" series. I couldn't be more excited to take this next journey.

I do want to once again introduce you to Andy Blanks who co-wrote "How To Be A Man: Pursuing Christ-Centered Masculinity" with me. Andy serves as the Publisher for Iron Hill Press. He and Dr. Bryan Gill (another powerful man with God-given talent to write the type of content that I would endorse and consume), have partnered

to write the second book in this line, and let me assure you it is once again, meat with zero fluff, designed to be consumed the way men learn and grow.

Jesus is the perfect model of masculinity. But He's not the only one. The Bible is full of compelling examples of men following after God. Our challenge is to learn from them, which is not a foreign concept to us. The undeniable truth is that we are influenced (both positively and negatively) by men in our life. Think of how many times you have caught yourself saying or reacting to something exactly the way your dad, grandfather, uncle, boss, coach, or teacher would have responded or reacted. Many people don't often think of the men of the Bible being men that can shape our lives. This is a big mistake.

There is no better teacher than a man who has already traveled your same path. It's invaluable to learn from another man who has gained wisdom by undertaking the journey ahead of you, warning you of the traps ahead and enlightening you to the proper paths to take — paths that lead to life, not destruction. God gave us the example of the men of the Bible to function in much the same way. These men challenge and convict us by their faith, while at the same time teaching us through their mistakes. Abraham, Joseph, Joshua, David, Elijah, John the Baptist, Peter, and Paul all serve as excellent examples of the power of God to transform lives, but also as examples of His incredible grace and mercy.

I continue to be moved and inspired by how God faithfully uses the first "How To Be A Man" book to challenge men all over the world. If you haven't read it yet, consider going back and reading it as well. But for now, take the challenge to learn from the real men of the Bible. As you accept this challenge, never lose sight that these men are just men; the only great thing about them is the God they serve. You too have access to that same power, but you must surrender your life to the Lord.

Are you willing to submit to the Lordship of Jesus Christ and become the kind of man that can only be accomplished through the transformation provided by the redeeming power of God through His Son Jesus Christ? Until you do, you will never be a real man.

Are you ready?

Rick Burgess
Co-host, The Rick and Bubba Show
New York Times Best-Selling Author
Birmingham, AL
2019

INTRODUCTION

Who are the men who have shaped your life?

When we look back over our lives, many of us can identify men who had an oversized impact on the people we are today. These men were our fathers, our grandfathers, our uncles, our brothers. They were men in our neighborhood. Or men from our churches. They were college roommates, or teammates, or co-workers. These individuals helped teach us what it meant to be the kind of man we are today.

We learned from their examples. We watched how they interacted with their wives. We watched the way they conducted themselves in public. We noticed how they dealt with tough situations. We watched them. And we learned.

They taught us to drive. They taught us how to shoot. They taught us how to take something apart and put it back together. They listened when we needed someone to listen to us. They disciplined us when we went astray. They laughed with us. Maybe they cried with us. They shepherded us, walking with us as we grew into the men we have become today.

These men, these examples, were not perfect. They made mistakes. They may have let us down. But they took the responsibility of their roles seriously, and they shaped our lives as a result. We are better off as a result of our lives having intersected with theirs.

As many of you read the previous paragraphs, you thought of the men in your life who had just such an impact on you. But how many of you thought about the men of the Bible? It's safe to say, probably not a lot. Which is a shame.

The Bible is the true Word of God. The people we meet in its pages are real people. They are not mythical characters. They are not made up creations. They are men and women who lived in specific times in specific locations. They are not two-dimensional people, as we sometimes make them out to be. They are complex human beings, just like the people you interact with every day. We can look at their lives and trust that what we are seeing is a snapshot of people who went about their days thousands of years ago much like we do today.

If we believe that the Bible was given to us by God and that it is the primary way He wants to show us Himself and His ways, then we have to believe we can learn from the stories of the people we read about in its pages. Especially the stories of the men of the Bible.

In the men of the Bible, we see an example of what it looks like to follow after God. We see men forced to grapple with their faith and how to live their lives in a world that often seems opposed to their values. We see them experiencing successes and failures. We see them taking stands for God. And we see them falling short of what God wants for them. In short, we see ourselves.

We can learn from the men in the Bible in the same way in which we have learned from the men in our lives.

The first book released in this line, *How To Be A Man: Pursuing Christ-centered Masculinity*, guided men to look to Jesus to define what it means to be a man. In Jesus, we see God as He was walking on this earth, fully God, fully man. Jesus is the ultimate example of what it means to be a man. The stories we heard after talking to men who had gone through the book were amazing. God is still using that book in powerful ways to challenge and convict men to be the men God desires them to be. We knew that we wanted to follow the first *How To Be A Man* book with a different book, one that still called men to embrace a biblical model for masculinity. We prayed and thought about what that book might look like.

It didn't take long for us to decide to focus on the men of the Bible. Through their stories, we learn so much about God and ourselves. Their faith challenges us, and their missteps convict us.

Deciding who to focus on was the hard part. We sat down with Rick Burgess, host of the nationally syndicated radio show *Rick and Bubba* and co-author of the first *How To Be A Man* book, and talked through the men of the Bible who had the most to teach us. We came up with a pretty good list. In this book, you'll study the lives of eight real men from the Bible, including:

- ABRAHAM
- JOSEPH
- JOSHUA
- DAVID
- ELIJAH
- JOHN THE BAPTIST
- PETER
- PAUL

By examining the lives these men lived, you'll be challenged to live a life of impact and influence, changing the world around you for the sake of the Gospel.

The world is in dire need of men to step up and live the life God intends them to live. All around us we see the effects of men who have chosen not to boldly pursue Christ. God has called you to Himself and placed you where you are so that He might work through you to bring glory to Himself. And yet, too many men aren't faithful in living out the role God has tasked them with. We're passionate about trying to challenge men to embrace God's call on their lives. It is our prayer that God will work through this book, and each book in the *How To Be A Man* line, to call His children to a kind of faith that shakes up the world around them.

On behalf of Rick, whose foreword sets an excellent tone for this book, and the entire YM360/Iron Hill Press team, we want to thank you for investing your time and spiritual energy in this book. It's our prayer that God would work through you to impact your world for Christ. Please don't hesitate to let us hear from you.

God Bless,

Andy Blanks and Bryan Gill

WEEK 1:

ABRAHAM

What's the craziest thing you've done in the name of love? Because let's be honest, it'll make you do crazy things, won't it?

I'm almost sure I've spent more money and more time for love than I have anything else. The list of things I've done just because I love my wife would be the length of my arm. Places I've been. Movies I've watched. Walls painted, and pictures hung. Every DIY known to man. All for love.

I love my daughters. And I've done more for them simply because I love them than I ever thought possible. My son is still just a little guy, but I imagine the same will be true for him, as well. Love is a great motivator when it comes to our wife and kids.

But what if I asked you to tell me how your love for God has motivated you to go to great lengths to serve Him? To obey Him? To see His will done in the world and your life? What would your story be? If you're Abraham, you'd have no problem answering that question. Abraham's love for God was the motivation for an incredible journey, one that would shape history.

Over the next five days, you're going to learn about Abraham's life and his faith. You're going to see that he was capable of tremendous trust in God but also capable of a surprising amount of doubt. And through examining Abraham's faith, you'll be challenged to examine your own and to consider just how far your faith in God will take you.

ABRAHAM DAY 1

SCRIPTURE PASSAGE: GENESIS 12:1-9

What's the most you've ever had riding on a risky decision?

In 2009, a friend and I started YM360 (the parent org under which Iron Hill Press publishes this book) from scratch. We had enough investor dollars raised to leave our jobs and build a website. But that was about it. We were launching a publishing company with nothing to sell and no one to sell it to. We had no database. No email list. Nothing.

What we did have were families, and mortgages, and car payments, and a million other needs. And let me tell you, those first few years were as lean as they come. Our families made huge sacrifices for us to step out on faith and give birth to a dream God had put on our hearts. Through God's unfailing faithfulness, the ministry has thrived. Looking back, we can see God's hand of providence over us the entire time. But during those early years, the risk still felt overwhelming at times.

Read Genesis 12:1-9. Here we see one of the foundational moments in all of the Bible. God called Abram, who would become known as Abraham, to be the father of a great nation. The nation in question was the Israelites, God's chosen people. When God tells Abraham "in you all the families of the earth shall be blessed," He is foreshadowing the salvation that would one day be offered through His Son, Jesus. Of course, the main issue here is that Abraham and Sarah were unable to have children. God's declaration that His mighty work of nation-building would pass directly through this old, childless couple was miraculous. It shows once again that there is nothing God can't accomplish. But for the purpose of this devotion, I want to focus on Abraham's response in verse 4.

Abraham risked everything to respond in faith to a call from God. If we're honest, the call itself was pretty vague. God didn't even tell Abraham where he would be going, only that He'd show him on the way. Scholars think Abraham was probably pretty well off. He uprooted all his people, all his flocks, everything, for the sake of obeying God's call. The question we have to ask ourselves is, what are we willing to risk to be obedient to God's call on our lives?

God's plan for you is probably not to build a nation out of your family. I mean, He could if He wanted to . . . But that's most likely not it. Rest assured, however, that God DOES have a plan for you. He knows you, and just like Abraham, He desires to work through you to accomplish His purposes. What you have to decide is whether or not you will listen and obey. Are you willing to put it all in God's hands and trust Him to lead you, no matter what?

LEARNING FROM ABRAHAM

1. How much weight do you give to your "security" or your "comfort"? How much do these concepts impact the decisions you make in your life?

2. Have you ever let your security or comfort impact the way you think about your faith? If you were to make a list of things that are too important to you to risk to follow God, what would that list look like? Feel free to use this space to write out your list.

3. When we put our comfort over God's call, we're saying that we know better than God about how best to use the life God's so graciously given us. What's wrong with this way of thinking?

4. When we look at Abraham and his response to God, it all comes down to trust. Ask yourself today, "How much do I trust God? Do I trust God enough to follow Him where He leads me?" Only you know the answer to this question. Spend some time in prayer today allowing God to reveal to you where your heart is when it comes to how much you trust Him.

ABRAHAM DAY 2

I struggle with patience. It's not that I'm impatient all the time. I'm pretty patient in a boat with a fishing rod, or in a tree stand with a rifle. But put me behind a slow driver in the fast lane, and my patience goes out the window.

Read all of Genesis 15. (It won't take you long, and it's an essential passage of the Bible.) Here we get a look at how God chooses to interact with people. God chooses to engage with Abraham in a way that honors God's perfect plan and addresses Abraham's imperfect faith. What we see at the beginning of this passage is Abraham asking questions about God's plans. He looked at God and said, "I continue childless." In other words, Abraham is impatient. He knows God has promised Him an heir. But at this time, God has not yet delivered.

I love seeing how God treated Abraham here. There were a lot of things He could have done. What He did is quite powerful. God showed Abraham the stars. God basically said, "If you can count these it will give you an idea of just how big your family will one day be." And something in the way God showed this to Abraham got his attention and assured him of God's promise. "And he believed the Lord."

But God wasn't done. What happens next seems kind of strange to our 21st-century understanding. God conducts a covenant ceremony. There were animal parts, and blood, and God represented as a smoking pot and a torch. What do we make of this? In its purest form, here is what is going on: this is God ratifying a covenant with Abraham in the manner that was customary during this time. For the sake of this devotion, don't get too caught up in how God went about it. Focus on what God did.

The eternal God of the universe, the perfect creator of all things, made a binding, eternal promise to one of His flawed, finite, created beings. Abraham didn't walk through the pieces of the animals. God did. God bound Himself to a promise to Abraham, and God always keeps His promises. Let that sink in. God does not see personally interacting with humanity as something to shy away from. He does not look at you and see someone to be avoided. God blesses us with His presence and His promises.

When we are tempted to be impatient with God's timeline, remember that just like His promises, His timing is perfect. God will always act for His glory and our good, in line with His perfect understanding of timing. That's a promise you can rely on.

LEARNING FROM ABRAHAM

1. Why is it so hard for us to wait on God? What does our tendency to rush God say about our faith in Him?

2. There are quite a few stories from Scripture of people waiting on God. Abraham would wait 25 years before Isaac, his son, was born. David would wait 15 years between the time God promised him that he would be king and when he actually took the throne. Simeon waited his whole life to see the Messiah. Why do you think God allows us to wait on Him to work? What is it about waiting that He finds so instructive?

3. We could spend a lot of time talking about the fact that God didn't ask Abraham to promise Him anything, but that God initiated this covenant with Abraham. What does God's faithfulness and His willingness to show Himself faithful to Abraham say about His faithfulness to you?

4. Spend some time today in prayer, thanking God for His faithfulness, and asking Him to grow in you the desire to wait patiently for His plan to come to fruition in your life.

SCRIPTURE PASSAGE: GENESIS 20

Read Genesis 20. And get ready: this isn't Abraham at his finest. Here we see Abraham telling Abimelech that Sarah was his sister, not his wife. Abraham had a bad habit of doing this; he did it three times over the course of traveling from Ur of the Chaldeans to the land of Canaan. He did this because he was scared that if the rulers of the lands he passed through knew Sarah was his wife, they'd kill him and take her as a concubine. If he lied and told them Sarah was his sister, these rulers would probably still take her as a concubine but wouldn't kill Abraham. (Still a pretty crummy deal for Sarah.) Abraham shows us here the very real truth that as men, we are prone to following hard after God one minute, and sinfully acting in our own self-interest the next.

What happened as a result of the lie Abraham told Abimelech? First, Abraham put Abimelech in the position of sinning in God's eyes. God had a disturbing heart-to-heart convo with Abimelech. God told Abimelech He'd kill him for taking Abraham's wife. As a result, Abimelech was understandably a little miffed at Abraham. Second, in his "apology," Abraham tips his hand that he underestimated the faithfulness of the people of the Negeb. Abraham assumed they didn't know God. Abimelech did. Abraham allowed his fears to get in the way of his faithfulness. Third, the brand of faith Abraham demonstrated for his wife was a far cry from the kind of faith a husband wants to model. Ultimately, Abraham showed a considerable lack of faith in God, in this instance and in the two other cases in which he pulled this ruse.

Abraham proved faithful in many aspects of the journey (both physical and spiritual) that God called him to undertake. After all, when God commanded, Abraham obeyed. But Abraham proved over and over that there were moments where even as he obeyed God's big-picture directives, he failed in dealing with the specific uncertainties of life like a man of God should.

When things got hairy, Abraham acted in cowardice. He put his well-being ahead of the wellbeing of those he loved. In doing so, he showed a lack of faith in God.

How we respond when we encounter obstacles goes a long way in defining our character. When life throws us a curveball, and we respond in faith, we honor both God and the people He has given us influence over. When we fail to seek God in the midst of trials, we not only fail God, but we can easily lead others in our lives to go astray as well. It's easy to respond in faith when the road is smooth. But when things get a little bumpy, the real depth of our faith is tested.

LEARNING FROM ABRAHAM

1. If you were to ask your wife and children, or maybe even your co-workers and friends, how you react in times of crisis, how do you think they might respond?

2. What does this say about your faith in God? Are you convicted by how you imagine they might respond? Or does it confirm the closeness of your relationship with God?

3. Remembering God's past faithfulness in times of trials goes a long way in how we handle trials in the future. Yet too many of us never stop long enough to recall how God saw us through the challenges we've faced in our lives. Stop now and reflect on some specific challenging times in your life and God's role during the midst of those trials. Write them down in the space provided if you want.

4. Now, spend some time thanking God in prayer for how He has walked with you in the midst of life's trials. Thank Him for never forsaking you and for acting within His goodness and mercy. Let this time of prayerful reflection strengthen and uphold you.

ABRAHAM DAY 4

Yesterday you read an account of Abraham modeling a fragile faith in the face of trials. Today, you're going to see Abraham demonstrating a level of faith in God that is so deep it's hard to put into words. But before you read, let's get caught up. Find Genesis 22 in your Bible or Bible app. At this point in the story, God has been faithful to Abraham. He and Sarah had a son, Isaac. This passage starts by telling us that some time has passed, and Isaac is most likely a young adult.

Now, read Genesis 22:1-14. Let's get straight to the question you're probably asking right now: Why would God have asked Abraham to sacrifice his child? It seems so un-Godlike, doesn't it? The answer is twofold. First, verse 1 tells us that God wanted to test Abraham's faith. God wanted to see what Abraham's first love was: Himself, or Isaac. Second, child sacrifice was something that was common in many of the pagan cultures in Abraham's time. It would have been a practice that, although horrific, would not have been unheard of to Abraham. Furthermore, God wasn't asking Abraham to do anything He wasn't willing to do, as He would prove one day on a cross at Calvary.

God tested Abraham to determine what Abraham valued more: the gift or the Giver. If God was going to set-up Abraham as the father of His people, He had to make sure Abraham was a man of undying affection for Him. God asked Abraham to sacrifice his son as a burnt offering, and amazingly, Abraham agreed. By doing so, he demonstrated a remarkable faith in God.

Abraham must have been heartbroken and distraught. Can you imagine the three-day journey to the mountain? Yet, even in verse 5 as they prepare to go up the mountain, Abraham tells his servants that he and Isaac will return. Abraham trusted God to relent or to find another way through it!

God did relent, making a way out for Isaac in the form of a ram in a thicket. The ram in this story foreshadows another time, on another hill, when God would miraculously provide the sacrifice that saved us from death. But at the heart of this story is a father who loved his son, and was willing to lose him for the sake of his trust in God.

As men living in a fast-paced world full of distractions, it's easy for us to underestimate God's desire for the full attention of our heart. God is not satisfied sharing your affection with anything else, whether that's your spouse, your kids, your career, or your hobbies. If God tested you today, what would you have a hard time withholding? What does that say about where your heart's affection lies?

LEARNING FROM ABRAHAM

1. Deep down, Abraham had faith in God's character. He showed in verse 5 that he believed that God would provide a way to save Isaac's life. Who is God to you? Do you know Him well enough to count on His goodness? In your own words, describe God's character in the space below.

2. What in your life competes with God for time and energy? Be honest.

3. What does it say about us as men that we are so quick to allow things to come between God and us? And why is it that so many of the things that we allow to come before our commitment to God have so little eternal value?

4. Here's a question for you to think about: What are you missing out by NOT allowing God to be the primary focus of your life? How might your vocation be different if God were your first priority? How might your marriage be different? What would your relationship with your children be like if you pursued God above all else? Maybe the biggest question is, "what are you waiting for"?

ABRAHAM DAY 5

The older I get, the more I think about the impact my life is having. I think this is something most men consider as they age. I find myself living with a greater sense of purpose. There is a genuine desire not to waste the time I have been given. I want my life to count for something. I want the impact of my life to be felt long after I leave this world. Can you relate?

The word legacy is a powerful word. It can also be an overwhelming concept. When we think about living a life that is so meaningful that its impact is felt long after we're gone, well, it can seem like a tall task. But I want to help you think about legacy in a way that is not quite so overwhelming.

A legacy is what happens when you string together a lifetime's worth of days spent living in the center of God's will. It's accomplished in day-sized chunks. It's merely a matter of faithfulness over time.

Read Genesis 25:7-11. This is the period at the end of Abraham's life story. Abraham lived a long, long life. By all accounts, he lived a full life. The biblical language here in these verses is rich with meaning. If you read it in its original Hebrew and from the perspective of the original cultural context, everything about these verses speaks to Abraham having lived a fulfilling, blessed life. He was able to experience the realization of God's call on his life. His two sons buried him in the land God had promised him would be his and his family's home. His life was complete, and while history recognizes that Abraham wasn't perfect, his legacy is one of faithfulness and steady obedience to the Lord.

Every day, you build your legacy. Every day, the things you do and the things you don't do shape the world around you. When it's all said and done, and you look back over your life, what will the final verdict be? Did you use your talents and time to advance God's Kingdom? Did you invest in the people you love? Did your life tell the story of God's faithfulness to you?

It's too late to wait until it's over to start building a legacy. Decide today that you're committed to making the most of what God has given you.

LEARNING FROM ABRAHAM

1. Think about the men in your life who left or will leave a powerful legacy. What impact have they had on you and those around them? In what ways did their lives bring glory to God?

2. If you had to put a number on your legacy with "0" representing a completely negative legacy and "10" representing an amazing one, where would you be? How do you feel about where you rate yourself?

3. Have you ever taken a moment to write out how you would like to be remembered by your family and those close to you? Try it now. It may seem awkward at first, but give it a shot. Think about the people in your life and write a sentence or two about how you'd like for them to remember you and the impact you made on them.

4. The exercise you just did should serve as a huge encouragement for you to think of your life in terms of daily faithfulness. Pray to God today, asking Him to convict you of any sin in your life. Ask Him to give you the strength to be the man you are called to be, today. Then live today for the Lord. When you wake up tomorrow, do the same thing. And don't stop.

WEEK 2:

JOSEPH

When you think of Joseph, several things probably come to mind: the coat of many colors, vivid dreams, perseverance, and Egypt to name a few. (Some of you just shouted, "Amazing Technicolor Dreamcoat!" But, I'm ignoring you, and we're not going there. Moving on . . .)

Joseph's story is legendary. Many people read his story and wish they could be like him. However, unlike Joseph, we have the benefit of seeing his journey from beginning to end. As a teenager, Joseph was given only a glimpse of what his life would become as an adult. He knew God had a plan for him but didn't know what his journey would entail. Like every other man, Joseph was only privy to the events of his life as they unfolded. He knew that he would be robed in fine linens as an adult but not that he would be stripped of his colorful robe as a young man. He saw his brothers bowing down to him on a throne as an adult, but not them peering down at him in a well. Through it all, Joseph had an uncanny way of staying the course and remaining faithful in each trial he faced. The result of his faithfulness was the salvation of a nation and the preservation of the lineage of Christ.

I want to do something unusual. Before you get started with this week's devotions, I want you to take a few minutes and read Genesis chapters 37 & 39 – 41. I know that seems like a lot, but I want us to start from a 30,000 ft. view and work our way down over the next five days. Also, let's recall Joseph's genealogy to give some background. God blessed Abraham with a son, Isaac. Isaac was the father of Jacob and Esau. Jacob, also called Israel, had twelve sons later known as the twelve tribes of Israel—one of whom was Joseph.

Joseph lived an extraordinary life and can teach us fascinating truths regarding biblical manhood. In the next five days, we are going to explore topics such as facing adversity, growing in wisdom and discernment, responding to temptations, embracing reconciliation, and the understanding the transforming power of reflection. Joseph gives solid examples of how real men of God should respond to each of these topics.

JOSEPH DAY I

SCRIPTURE PASSAGE: GENESIS 39:1-4; 19-21; 40:12-14, 23; 41:37-43

Do you remember the fuss surrounding Y2K? Those who claimed to know the future said the world would end at midnight on January 1, 2000. Others thought computers would not be able to roll over to account for the year 2000 and that everything from microwaves to missile silos would stop working. People were losing their minds over the impending doom. Even the name, Y2K, was ominous.

My dad and I were sitting in our house in south Alabama watching the ball drop in Times Square that New Year's Eve. Neither of us had bought into the hype. The ball dropped, the countdown hit zero, and our house immediately went dark. "This is it. It's happening!" I ran through the house knocking over lamps, stepping on dogs, and busting my shin . . . only to find the world had not ended. Instead, a drunk driver had hit the power pole at the end of my street causing the power to go out. So much for predicting the future.

Read the following verses: Genesis 39:1-4; 19-21; 40:12-14, 23; 41:37-43. As a seventeen-year-old, God gave Joseph a couple of dreams that foretold his future. However, he wasn't given a map that would reveal each step along the way; he only knew the end would work out fine.

Joseph's life repeated itself this way: something terrible happened, he trusted God, God delivered him, repeat. Joseph went from being Jacob's favored son to being sold into slavery, accused of raping his master's wife, sentenced to prison, then finally made second in command over all of Egypt. If you only look at Joseph's circumstances, he had every right to be angry and bitter against his brothers, Potiphar's wife, the cupbearer, and even God. He could've thought, "Why is this happening to me? You said you had a plan for me!" But he didn't say that.

When we look at Joseph's responses rather than his circumstances, we see a man of God, full of grace, faithful, and unshaken by his environment. Joseph focused on God even when his life was spiraling out of control. He didn't let the bumps in the road stop him in his tracks.

When your business relocates, and you're faced with the choice of moving or taking the severance (if there even is one), will you make the best of the situation? When you're falsely accused of something, will you trust that God knows the truth? When the boss' nephew gets the promotion, how will you respond? Men of God believe the promise that there is hope in the end regardless of the bumps along the way. Your task is to focus on God rather than the situation, keep striving to love others, avoid bitterness, and trust that God's plan for your life will eventually bring Him glory.

LEARNING FROM JOSEPH

1. When you read the story of Joseph's life, which part resonated with you the most?

2. Think of a time in your life when you got the raw end of the deal. Now answer these questions:
   a. How did you respond?
   b. Did your response align with what you believe about God?
   c. What would you have done differently?

3. As men, we often get frustrated when things don't work out the way we envisioned it. We also don't like to admit when we're frustrated; that would mean talking about feelings and who has time for that? But humor me for a minute and try to recall a time when you felt frustrated because a situation turned out differently than you imagined it. Now, try to identify God's hand in that situation. How did God specifically reveal Himself and His plan to you?

4. Spend some time in prayer thanking God for His hand over your life in the midst of tough times. Confess any frustration you've felt with God. (It's OK. He's big enough to handle it.) Ask the Holy Spirit to work in your life to give you the strength and wisdom to deal with disappointment in the way Joseph did.

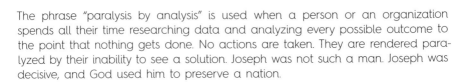

JOSEPH DAY 2

SCRIPTURE PASSAGE: GENESIS 41:25-35

The phrase "paralysis by analysis" is used when a person or an organization spends all their time researching data and analyzing every possible outcome to the point that nothing gets done. No actions are taken. They are rendered paralyzed by their inability to see a solution. Joseph was not such a man. Joseph was decisive, and God used him to preserve a nation.

Read Genesis 41:25-35. After interpreting the dreams of the chief cupbearer and chief baker, Joseph stayed in prison for two more years. Until one day, Pharaoh had a series of dreams no one could interpret. The chief cupbearer finally remembered Joseph's ability and told Pharaoh. Pharaoh then summoned Joseph to interpret his dreams. Joseph told Pharaoh there would be seven years of plenty and seven years of famine. But, the famine would be so severe that the seven years of plenty would be forgotten unless they acted.

Joseph told Pharaoh he needed to find a man who was "wise and discerning" (Gen. 41:33) and put him in charge of the day-to-day operations of Egypt. Joseph looked at the situation: the whole land was on the brink of seven years of famine. Seven years! There's mass hysteria at my house if my kids go seven minutes without something to eat. However, Joseph didn't panic. He immediately thought of a plan and confidently gave his recommendation. That's the kind of person I want working for me. And evidently, that's the kind of man Pharaoh was looking for as well. Right there on the spot, he promoted Joseph from prisoner to second in command over all of Egypt.

Men of God should be wise and discerning in all areas of their life: home, community, church, and the workplace. Does your wife see you as active or passive? How about your kids? Men, you should be the one leading your family, not the one just along for the ride. With regards to your community, are you a nuisance on your street or are you someone your neighbors can look to for help? How about your workplace? You don't have to be the boss to be wise and discerning. Joseph wasn't the top dog, but he displayed the traits of a godly man. What about at your church? When someone asks for help, do you step up regardless of how menial the task or do you wait for a more glamorous position of influence to pitch in? Wise and discerning men serve without the promise of recognition. How about you?

LEARNING FROM JOSEPH

1. Think of a man in your life whom you consider wise and discerning. What qualities did/does he possess that you want to imitate in your own life?

2. It's not like you can run down to the convenient store and pick up a couple of bags of wisdom and discernment. So, how do you become wise and discerning as a man of God?

3. What is the hardest part of being wise and discerning? What responsibilities does it add to your life?

4. Have you ever prayed for wisdom? The Bible tells us that if we ask for wisdom God is faithful and will make us wise. Do you trust God to grow this trait in you? Begin to pray for wisdom and to watch for how God is answering this prayer.

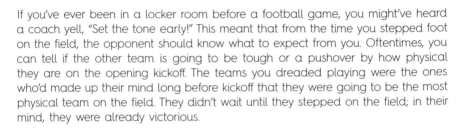

JOSEPH DAY 3

SCRIPTURE PASSAGE: GENESIS 39:6-20

If you've ever been in a locker room before a football game, you might've heard a coach yell, "Set the tone early!" This meant that from the time you stepped foot on the field, the opponent should know what to expect from you. Oftentimes, you can tell if the other team is going to be tough or a pushover by how physical they are on the opening kickoff. The teams you dreaded playing were the ones who'd made up their mind long before kickoff that they were going to be the most physical team on the field. They didn't wait until they stepped on the field; in their mind, they were already victorious.

Read Genesis 39:6-20. Joseph was probably around seventeen or eighteen years old when he was put in charge of Potiphar's house. The Bible tells us that he was a good-looking young man, and Potiphar's wife noticed. Day after day, this woman approached him and day after day, Joseph denied her advances. Potiphar's wife grew frustrated one day and grabbed Joseph and demanded he have sex with her. The Bible says, "he left his garment in her hand and fled and got out of the house."

Joseph knew the correct response to temptation was to flee. He knew he needed to do more than "just say no." Joseph's response to temptation was to get out of there as fast as he could, even if it meant running through the house naked. And he didn't stop when the temptation was out of sight; he ran out of the house where she lurked.

Somewhere along the way, purity became something reserved for women and children. This couldn't be further from the truth. As men of God, we should "set the tone early" with our response to sin and how we chase purity. The devil should shudder at the thought of tempting you because you have already made your mind up to resist his attacks.

Men of God drastically resist temptation and chase purity. They take the extra steps around the office to avoid the receptionist with the low-cut blouse. They have porn-blocking software on your phone and computer. They go a different way home, so they don't have to drive by her house. Seem drastic? It should be; it's that important.

Just like with Joseph, the devil is going to attack you with the one thing that is forbidden—your very own Potiphar's wife. How will you respond? You better decide now, or it will be too late when that temptation hits. Joseph didn't decide to resist temptation the moment he was tempted; his mind was made up long before he stepped on the field.

LEARNING FROM JOSEPH

1. What guardrails have you put in your life to help you resist temptation?

2. I'm sure a personal sin came to mind as you read this devotional. How could you do a better job of resisting that specific temptation in the future?

3. Think of a time in your life when you were proud of how you dealt with temptation in your life.
    a. What was different about your life when you successfully resisted that temptation?
    b. Were you in an accountability group? Were you studying your Bible more consistently? Were you praying more?
    c. What was different and how can you get back to that man who was more effective at resisting temptation?

JOSEPH DAY 4

SCRIPTURE PASSAGE: GENESIS 44:30-34

It can be rough when a family's patriarch or matriarch dies, and the survivors are left to fight over the inheritance. Anger and bitterness grow each year that passes and before you know it, decades have slipped away without siblings speaking to each other. All for what? A few extra dollars or possessions you didn't earn anyway?

Joseph knew the value of reconciliation. He knew what it felt like to be the outcast of the family and banished from his siblings. When the famine spread to Canaan, Joseph's brothers visited Egypt looking for food. Joseph recognized his brothers, and it was an emotional reunion for him, but he chose to conceal his identity until a vital thing happened—reconciliation.

Joseph knew his younger brother, Benjamin, was in danger of suffering the same fate of being ostracized as he was years ago. Joseph wanted to be sure his brothers were united and reconciled to each other before he revealed himself to them. So Joseph decided to test his brothers. After slipping a silver cup into Benjamin's bag of food and threatening to enslave him for thievery, Joseph saw a contrite heart within Judah, the same spokesman of the group who had convinced his brothers to sell Joseph into slavery (instead of murdering him) twenty years earlier.

Read Genesis 44:30-34. Judah pled with Joseph even to the point of being willing to give his own life for Benjamin. Can you imagine what was going through Joseph's mind as Judah was advocating for Benjamin? "Where were you when I needed you in the bottom of a well? Why weren't you my advocate like you are now?" No, Joseph didn't say any of that. He was a man of God, and men of God value reconciliation. As he watched his brother's passionate plea for Benjamin's protection, I imagine Joseph saying is, "OK. Now you're ready. Now it's my turn to be reconciled to you." What we see next in Genesis 45 is an awesome reunion full of grace and love and forgiveness and salvation.

Men of God value relationships and fight for reconciliation. Men of God are the first to offer an olive branch or peace offering to save a relationship over winning at all costs and driving a wedge between you and your neighbor. It is more important to be righteous and save a relationship than it is to be right and burn a bridge. God values relationships more than he values victories. Men of God should have the same zeal for relationships as God.

LEARNING FROM JOSEPH

1. What evidence in your life would prove that you value relationships?

2. Think of someone in your life with whom you need to be reconciled. What barriers are stopping you from making things right with them? Circle the words that come to mind.
   - Stubbornness
   - Pride
   - Hurt
   - Apathy
   - Feeling wronged
   - Shame
   - Guilt
   - Lack of effort
   - Waiting for forgiveness
   - Lack of grace
   - Lack of love

3. God wants us to be reconciled to each other and Himself. Take time right now to either schedule a phone call, write a letter, or plan a visit with whomever it is you need to be reconciled.

4. For many men, if you are honest, you don't want reconciliation. You're still feeding past wrongs. What you don't realize is that this is poisoning you. If your heart is far from wanting reconciliation, commit to praying to God and asking Him to work on making your heart more like His. Listen to what He wants to tell you about His love for reconciliation.

JOSEPH DAY 5

SCRIPTURE PASSAGE: GENESIS 50:15-21

Do you journal? Or do you think it's something only teenage girls do? The value of journaling is that it forces you to document moments of reflection. Even if you don't like to journal, reflection is one of the most valuable tools a man of God has at his disposal.

Reflection is a powerful thing. It gives you the chance to see the big picture and identify what you did wrong or right and how you can change next time. You may know reflection by another name: debriefing after a mission, reviewing case studies, analyzing a profit and loss report, watching game film. You reflect on what happened to get a better grasp of what really happened.

Read Genesis 50:15-21. When we look at the end of Joseph's story, I'm convinced Joseph spent a lot of time reflecting. Whether or not he journaled is unknown, but reflection is certain. One of the most powerful statements in the Old Testament is contained within this passage, "What you meant for evil, God meant for good." Can you imagine what it took for Joseph to get to that point of acceptance? That kind of outlook doesn't happen overnight. For Joseph to get to the point where he saw God's hand in every lousy event, he must have spent years reflecting.

Think about Joseph's life. God prepared him to deal with each trial by how He delivered him from the previous one. Joseph learned perseverance and God's provision each step of the way. Whether Joseph was in the bottom of a well, a cage in a caravan, the depths of a prison, or the middle of a famine, God was with Joseph. Joseph grew to trust God after each event and faced the next trial with confidence because of what God had previously done.

Men of God trust God in every trial because they recognize each previous instance where God provided. If your faith is weak, maybe you haven't spent enough time reflecting on God's provision in your life to this point. Reflection is a surefire way to strengthen your faith. God is unchanging and cares for his children. Do you trust that?

If you are fired from work, and it sends you spiraling out of control, think about how God has provided for you in the past. Thank Him for the unknown way He is shaping you. If you get a grim diagnosis from the doctor, reflect on how God has prepared you for this battle. Don't ask God "why" something bad happens to you, ask him "how." "How are you going to use this for your glory, God?" God allows us to reflect on our past to reassure us of our future.

LEARNING FROM JOSEPH

1. Take a few minutes to reflect on a time when God took a bad situation and turned it into a good one. Finish this sentence with a few words that will help you remember it, "It was that time when _____ happened."

2. How did God use that situation for good?

3. Where did you see God's grace in that situation?

4. In what way did God grow you through that situation?

5. Whether or not you want to realize it, you just journaled. Try using this format to guide your daily or weekly reflections. Identify the Good, Grace, and Growth areas of a situation and document what you find. Try it for a few days, then figure out a schedule that works for you to be more consistent.

WEEK 3:
JOSHUA

Years ago, when my wife and I were first married, we'd go dancing at a country club my wife's grandparents were members of. We'd eat dinner and spend the evening dancing (or trying to in my case) to the music from the 10-piece band playing jazz and big-band classics from the '40s and '50s. We had a blast. The band was led by Mr. George, a slight gentleman pushing eighty years old. George was always smiling as he led the band through their paces. His white, wispy hair was mostly gone on top, and he was a little stooped over, but he had this great handlebar mustache that accentuated his trumpet playing perfectly.

One night while we were eating, my wife's grandfather, Neal, called Mr. George over to our table. Neal had been a decorated Marine Corp artillery officer during WWII and Korea. He was a prominent attorney and a larger than life figure in my eyes. That's why I was surprised when I sensed a little bit of awe in his voice when he introduced me to Mr. George. "Andy," Neal said, "would you ever guess that George landed on Normandy Beach as an 18-year old and was in Paris when the Germans surrendered"? Being a Marine and a WWII history buff, I was all in. We sat for the next half hour as Mr. George regaled us with stories of chasing the Nazis across Europe, and of coming home and playing trumpet up and down the east coast in legendary bands. We were mesmerized. This unassuming man had lived a storybook life, and we were probably the only people in the crowded ballroom that even knew it.

I think Joshua and Mr. George have something in common (outside of the fact that they were both pretty awesome soldiers). I think Joshua's amazing life is "hidden in plain sight" from many Christians. Joshua was a remarkable person who lived an epic story. And yet, I think this gets lost sometimes. Joshua gets overshadowed by Moses in the story of Israel's history. And while Moses is rightfully a more significant character in the overall biblical narrative, if you've ever really dug in and studied Joshua, you'll agree with me that in many ways, Joshua stepped in and completed the task Moses couldn't.

If you've never really studied Joshua's life, I am excited to introduce you to him. While we don't have time to cover everything he experienced, I think you're going to quickly realize based on the moments we're going to study that few people in the Bible are as faithful, capable, and courageous as Joshua. You're going to love this guy. I believe he has a TON to teach us about what it means to live and lead as men of God.

So let's turn the page and get started.

JOSHUA DAY 1

Recently I was raking leaves when my five-year-old son asked if he could help me. He came out, grabbing a small rake from our garage. Now, let me set the stage: it was cold and drizzling, and there was a mountain of leaves. The weather had been bad the previous two weekends, so this was a beast of a task. I fully expected him to bail out after a couple of minutes, and if he had, it would have been fine. Except that he didn't.

For the next half hour, he and I raked together, talking back and forth as we went. He finally got wet and cold enough to go inside, but within about 15 minutes he was back sitting on the porch, PB and J in hand, carrying on a steady stream of conversation with me. For whatever reason, on this particular day, he wasn't going to be happy unless he was with me. He needed to be where I was (and I didn't mind one bit).

Take a moment and read Exodus 24:12-18 and Exodus 33:7-11. I want you to read both of these passages, though I want us to focus on the second one. Here are two snapshots of incredible moments in young Joshua's life (he was probably in his mid to late 20s). He was with Moses on the top of Mount Sinai when God gave Moses the Ten Commandments, and he was with Moses when Moses would go to meet with God outside the camp. These instances had to be extremely formative for Joshua, shaping his faith and his character as a leader. But for this devotion, I want to focus on his actions in Exodus 33.

First, picture in your mind what this looked like. Far outside the camp of the people, Moses had set up a tent where he and others would go to seek God. That this tent was outside the camp signifies God's holiness, His "otherness." He wasn't physically among the people because He is not of the people. But He was with the people because of the covenant relationship He had instituted with Israel. When Moses met with God, God would appear in a pillar of cloud. Each time this happened, Joshua was there by Moses' side, taking it all in, watching Moses interact with God, and learning how God communicated with Moses.

When it was over, Moses would leave. But not Joshua. At the end of these times of meeting, Joshua hung back, unwilling to depart just yet. In these moments, we see Joshua, decades before he would take leadership of Israel, laying the foundation for a steadfast commitment to God. For whatever reason, Joshua lingered, unwilling to move on. He wasn't going to be satisfied unless he could spend just a little longer in the presence of the Lord.

As we seek to learn from the men of the Bible, this seems like a trait worth imitating.

LEARNING FROM JOSHUA

1. I want you to pause for a moment and think about your attitude toward spending time with God, whether in prayer or Bible reading or both. Is it something you look forward to? Can you relate to Joshua's desire to not depart from God's presence? Take a minute and consider this.

2. If you find that you can't relate to Joshua's desire to remain in God's presence, why do you think this is? List a few of the obstacles that you believe keep you from having a stronger desire to spend time with God.

3. Many Christian men live their lives without a habit of spending meaningful time in Bible reading and prayer. The truth about these men is that they are blowing it. Big time. You cannot follow what you don't know. You cannot teach your children to value things you don't value. Don't pass over what I am about to say: it is VITAL that you cultivate the desire to know God and to spend time in His presence. Look back at your list of obstacles. Identify one or two that you can eliminate (or at least reduce the impact of) today. Make a plan to make a change, and commit to following through.

4. If you need to, spend time in prayer right now asking God to forgive you for the sin of spiritual laziness. Ask God to convict you and empower you through His Spirit that lives in you. Pray that God would give you the strength to re-discover your passion for knowing Him, and to develop a Joshua-like hunger for Him.

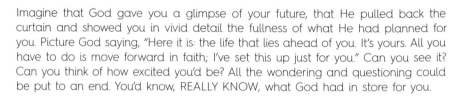

JOSHUA DAY 2

Imagine that God gave you a glimpse of your future, that He pulled back the curtain and showed you in vivid detail the fullness of what He had planned for you. Picture God saying, "Here it is: the life that lies ahead of you. It's yours. All you have to do is move forward in faith; I've set this up just for you." Can you see it? Can you think of how excited you'd be? All the wondering and questioning could be put to an end. You'd know, REALLY KNOW, what God had in store for you.

But then imagine that those around you - your friends, your family - shouted you down. "Yeah, that snapshot God gave you looked really cool, but c'mon . . . There's NO WAY you can accomplish that. It's way too hard to get there from here!" Imagine that no matter what you said and no matter how strong your faith in God was, the people you trusted the most couldn't bear to see you embrace the vision. What's more, imagine they get furious with you for even wanting to consider moving forward in faith. They want to kill you.

With this in mind, read Numbers 13 and 14. Moses had led the Israelites out of slavery in Egypt toward the land God had promised them. They were standing on the border, about to embrace God's plan. God led Moses to send men to scout out the land to formulate a plan to take it. The problems started when they came back.

Each of the men reported that the land God had promised them was amazingly fruitful, and all but two of these men said there was NO CHANCE they were going back. Too many obstacles. Too much to be afraid of. Too many questions. The God who had miraculously delivered them from slavery and parted the Red Sea surely wasn't powerful enough to overcome the challenges they saw. The verdict was clear: "We're in big trouble."

But wait! Caleb and Joshua had different thoughts. "We got this! Remember this is God's promise, guys. Don't be afraid! This is God's plan for us, His people!" And with that, everyone agreed and went in to possess the land. Right? Wrong. When Caleb and Joshua tried to convince the people to act in faith, their friends and family members wanted to kill them. Talk about a bad day.

As we're about to see, there were MAJOR consequences for the Israelite's doubt. But what about Joshua? What must it have been like to see God's promise, and to know that the God who promised it could see it through, but to have a tide of doubters act against you? If you've ever faced ridicule or shame from others over your faith in God, you know what Joshua felt like. Let's take some time to unpack how we might learn from Joshua's experience in the face of such a great crisis.

LEARNING FROM JOSHUA

1. Reread Numbers 14:1-10. What confusion and frustration Joshua and Caleb must have felt! They saw the situation so clearly, so correctly. But look at the despair and the hysteria of the people who had completely lost faith in God. Examine yourself. Do you have the faith of Joshua? Could you stand boldly for what you KNOW is right in the face of withering criticism? How do you think Joshua and Caleb were able to do so?

2. There were severe consequences for those who doubted God's ability to deliver them: "[28] Say to them, 'As I live, declares the LORD, what you have said in my hearing I will do to you: [29] your dead bodies shall fall in this wilderness, and of all your number, listed in the census from twenty years old and upward, who have grumbled against me, [30] not one shall come into the land where I swore that I would make you dwell, except Caleb the son of Jephunneh and Joshua the son of Nun" (Numbers 14:28-30). God had done so much for the people. He had miraculously delivered them from slavery. He had shown them signs and wonders. And still, they rejected Him. Not only would entire generations of them not ever see the land God promised, but they would die after spending the rest of their lives wandering in the wilderness. How do you process God's punishment of the people? What does this say to you about God's holiness?

3. Joshua and Caleb would one day experience the land God promised them. But not without much hardship. As a man seeking to be who God has called you to be, what is your posture as you lead others through disappointment? In what ways is your attitude tied to who you know God to be?

4. Who are you to those around you? Are you the voice of the 10 Doubters? Do you allow perceived hardships to distract you from who God is? Or are you the voice of Joshua who never lost sight of the One who is capable of overcoming all things to accomplish His plan? Spend some time in prayer asking God to give you the voice of one who is grounded in the knowledge that God goes before you, always.

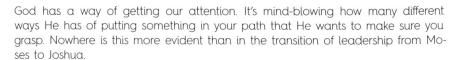

JOSHUA DAY 3

SCRIPTURE PASSAGE: DEUTERONOMY 31:7-8,
JOSHUA 1:1-9 AND JOSHUA 1:18

God has a way of getting our attention. It's mind-blowing how many different ways He has of putting something in your path that He wants to make sure you grasp. Nowhere is this more evident than in the transition of leadership from Moses to Joshua.

Read Deuteronomy 31:7-8, Joshua 1:1-9, and Joshua 1:18. Where we pick up the story, it is time for Moses to begin to hand over the leadership of Israel. The punishment of the 40 years of wandering was almost over. God was preparing to fulfill His promise to the people and He told Moses to take Joshua, his longtime assistant, and commission him in the sight of the people as the new leader of Israel.

In Deuteronomy 31:7-8, when Moses commissioned Joshua in front of the people, he told Joshua to "be strong and courageous . . . Do not fear or be dismayed." In Joshua 1:1-9, God reiterates this message Himself. He urges Joshua to "Be strong and courageous . . . Just as I was with Moses, so I will be with you . . . Be strong and courageous . . . Only be strong and very courageous . . . Have I not commanded you? Be strong and courageous. Do not be frightened, and do not be dismayed." Starting to see a pattern? Finally, we see the people saying this to Joshua as part of the ceremony solidifying his place as their leader: "Only be strong and courageous" (Joshua 1:18). Can you picture Joshua? "Alright, God! I got it. Be strong and courageous! Roger that!"

Was Joshua timid? Weak? A coward? We know for a fact that Joshua was a bold, fearless person, and would prove as much during his time as leader of the Israelites. So what do we make of this continued emphasis on strength, faith, and courage? First, these are vital traits of any leader. Strength of character, strength of will, fearlessness in the face of daunting tasks, the courage to do the right thing, steadfastness; each of these things are essential qualities in people who have a desire to lead, especially men who want to lead as God intends them to. Second, these qualities are being highlighted because Moses often failed to exhibit them.

Moses showed himself to be a man of God. That was never in doubt. And yet, over and over again, even in the midst of his many "successes" as a leader, Moses seemed to be unable at times to lead Israel boldly. Joshua, on the other hand, would be the man who led the people into the land God promised them. What's more, he would lead Israel for nearly forty years virtually without a blemish.

Joshua accepted the mantle of leadership and did so by embracing the call to be strong and brave. Let's look to Joshua and accept the challenge to lead in the same way.

LEARNING FROM JOSHUA

1. As God was preparing Joshua to lead, He had a message for him. Have you asked God what His message is to you? As you lead your family, as you lead those at your work, as you strive to be a leader in your church and community, what does God want you to focus on? Ask God to reveal this to you.

2. Steadfastness is one of the main traits that seem to be missing from many men in our culture. As someone who is striving to grow into the man God has called you to be, how are you doing in the area of steadfastness? How is your boldness these days? Do you find yourself shrinking from identifying as a Christ-follower? What work do you have to do in this area?

3. There is a moment in Joshua's time as a leader, not too long after this account, where we see him come very close to being "dismayed." In Joshua 7, Achan disobeys God's command not to plunder Jericho, and as a result, Israel experiences a rare military defeat in their next battle. After the defeat, Joshua falls on his face, tears his clothes, and cries out to God "Why have you brought us here just to let us fail"? God's response is almost comical: "The LORD said to Joshua, "Get up! Why have you fallen on your face?" He goes on to tell Joshua that Achan has sinned by keeping some of the plunder from Jericho. God basically says, "Hey, settle down. Get up, go deal with the issue, and let's move on with the plan." It's the closest we see Joshua come to making a misstep. Why is it so easy for us to get overwhelmed by the circumstances of life and lose sight of the fact that God is in control? What assurance can you take in God's response to Joshua?

4. Pray today for the strength of character and conviction. Pray for boldness. Pray for a confidence born out of knowing who God is and what He is capable of. Embrace God's desire to create these traits in you.

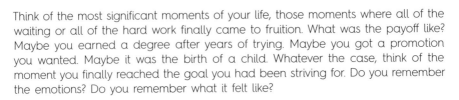

JOSHUA DAY 4

Think of the most significant moments of your life, those moments where all of the waiting or all of the hard work finally came to fruition. What was the payoff like? Maybe you earned a degree after years of trying. Maybe you got a promotion you wanted. Maybe it was the birth of a child. Whatever the case, think of the moment you finally reached the goal you had been striving for. Do you remember the emotions? Do you remember what it felt like?

Where we pick up Joshua's story today, the Israelites were on the precipice of one of these moments. For 400 hundred years they were enslaved in Egypt until God miraculously engineered their freedom. Then for 40 years, they had wandered in the desert, experiencing God's judgment for their rebellion. But now, the day had come. With Joshua at their head, the Israelites prepared to step into the Promised Land. And to mark the occasion, God made it known He wasn't done showing up and showing out. In a scene reminiscent of God's intervention at the Red Sea, God parted the flood-swollen Jordan River, and the entire nation of Israel passed through on dry ground to set foot for the first time on the land God had promised them. It was the powerful fruition of a generations-old promise from God. God had delivered His covenant people into the land He had set aside for them. It was a monumental day.

Read Joshua 4:4-7. This is a profound passage that has a ton of relevance for us as modern-day believers. Joshua asked a representative from each of the tribes of Israel to get a large stone from the middle of the Jordan and to make an altar on the other side. Joshua explained the purpose for this command: Years later when the people were walking down by the Jordan, and their children saw the monument, they would remember and pass along the stories of God's faithfulness.

The act of remembering is a powerful concept throughout the Bible. Over and over again, we see someone make an altar or monument to remember a specific interaction with God. The psalms are full of passages that call Israel to remember God's faithfulness in the past. As Christian men, we would do well to incorporate this practice in our lives and in the lives of those we're tasked with leading.

How well do you model Joshua's heart here? Do you make an effort to remind yourself and those around you of how God has interacted with you in the past? If not, your faith-life is missing a valuable spiritual practice. Remembering how God has intervened in your life creates an attitude of gratefulness. It reminds you of the foundation of faithfulness that your life is built on. Let's be challenged by Joshua. Let's be men who remember. And let's start today.

LEARNING FROM JOSHUA

1. This is your chance to remember times in your life where God has intervened or provided for you in ways only He can. Spend some time reflecting on your life. In the space provided below, write down some of these times. (Resist the urge to pass over this activity. This is important. You're not too busy. Stop and think about the ways God has impacted your life in the past.)

2. Now, even if this is something you're not used to doing, write down a prayer of thanks to God for how He has provided for you and led you in the past. Express your gratitude to Him in however you see fit. No one will see this but you and God.

3. Finally, this is important: Choose some way today of physically reminding your-self of God's faithfulness in the past. This could be as simple as picking up a rock from your driveway or yard and carrying it around in your pocket. It could be changing your screensaver on your phone to a Bible verse. It could be writing a word or phrase on a notecard and placing it on your bathroom mirror or your car's dashboard. Whatever you choose, make a physical reminder of God's faith-fulness and carry it around with you today. When you see it throughout the day, remember how much God loves you and how He desires to intervene in our lives for His glory and our good.

4. BONUS: If you have children, consider how you might tell them a story of how God intervened in your life. Explain to them that this is something you've been studying and you want them to know the kinds of ways that God takes care of His people.

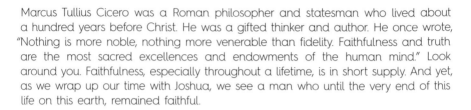

JOSHUA DAY 5

Marcus Tullius Cicero was a Roman philosopher and statesman who lived about a hundred years before Christ. He was a gifted thinker and author. He once wrote, "Nothing is more noble, nothing more venerable than fidelity. Faithfulness and truth are the most sacred excellences and endowments of the human mind." Look around you. Faithfulness, especially throughout a lifetime, is in short supply. And yet, as we wrap up our time with Joshua, we see a man who until the very end of this life on this earth, remained faithful.

In the final chapter of Joshua, we see the aged leader reminding the people of their binding covenant with God. Through Joshua, God recounts all that He has done for Israel. God essentially recalls the history of His relationship with them, from Abraham's calling to their deliverance from Egypt, up until the current moment they are standing on land God had promised ages ago.

Read Joshua 24:14-15. In verse 14, we see an ultimatum from an old man who is thinking about his legacy and wanting to get his house in order. Joshua is calling the people to remember their covenant relationship with God and to commit to following Him wholly and faithfully. Joshua makes it clear where his allegiance lies: "Now therefore fear the LORD and serve him in sincerity and in faithfulness. Put away the gods that your fathers served beyond the River and in Egypt, and serve the LORD. And if it is evil in your eyes to serve the LORD, choose this day whom you will serve, whether the gods your fathers served in the region beyond the River, or the gods of the Amorites in whose land you dwell. But as for me and my house, we will serve the LORD." Just 15 verses later, we learn that at the venerable age of 110, Joshua dies. His watch is over. His work is done. And as much as anyone we meet in Scripture, to the very end, Joshua stands unwavering in his steadfast commitment to serving God.

Nearing the end of his time on earth, Joshua could say without hesitation where his heart was. Joshua knew the cultural pressures Israel faced to follow the false gods of the nations surrounding them. Joshua stood tall and challenged them to serve the one, true God, just like he and his family did. The cool thing was that Joshua didn't have to run and check with his wife and kids. He could speak for his family because he led his family.

Joshua faithfully steered his family toward a faithful walk with the Lord. Can you say the same?

LEARNING FROM JOSHUA

1. If someone were to ask you if your family faithfully served God, how would you respond?

2. If you have a wife and children, what is your role in steering them away from the elements of our culture that fight for their heart's affection? How aware are you of the temptations and issues your children struggle with? What about your wife? In what ways do you help guide and lead her closer to God?

3. One of the most damaging postures a man can take is to be distracted or disengaged. There is no excuse for allowing things to happen under your roof that you are unaware of. Joshua could confidently speak for the attitude of his family's devotion toward God. Stop and spend a moment in reflection: Where do you spend your emotional energy? Is it engaging in the lives of your wife and children? Or is it spent at the office, the ballfield, or on personal hobbies? Let this be a gut-check for you. If you can't boldly and confidently speak for the spiritual state of your family, you have work you need to do.

4. Spend some time in prayer seeking God's guidance when it comes to your family. Ask Him to give you the strength to be a powerful presence in their lives. Ask Him to convict you in this area, convincing you that you are His provision for the people He has entrusted to your care.

WEEK 4:
DAVID

Some men in the Bible serve as models for us to follow with their example of character and actions. Some are good examples of what not to do. And there are others still who give us a glimpse into our own life, like a reflection in a mirror. David is unique in that he is all three of these wrapped into a very complicated and multi-layered individual.

David was a shepherd, a warrior, a poet, a musician, a king, and a father. He was also an adulterer, a murderer, a coward, and a liar. However, in the Book of Acts, David is referred to as a man after God's own heart. Like I said: complicated.

There will be times as you read about David's life when you will cheer him on and aspire to be like him. There will be times when you will want to punch him in the face because he is so stupid. And there may be sobering times of conviction where you will see a vivid reflection of your own life staring back at you through the pages of Scripture. Keep your pen or pencil beside you and jot down these moments when you see yourself.

David is a familiar man whose life is an open book. We know so much about him from what was written in the historical books of the Bible as well as his innermost thoughts found in the psalms. David is the second most referenced name in the Bible (second only to Jesus). But, as you read the scriptures over the next five days, I want you to read them slowly. Don't skim over some of the details because of the story's familiarity. Pretend that you don't know what you think you know and approach each day with a fresh set of eyes.

As you will see, David was a man of God despite his many flaws. I think it is easier to relate to David than other men in the Bible, like Joseph or Joshua, who never seemed to do any wrong. David did plenty wrong. He messed up several times in significant ways, but he showed us that through God's forgiveness and grace, even an adulterous murderer could be restored to be used by God.

DAVID DAY 1

SCRIPTURE PASSAGE: 1 SAMUEL 17:32-37

The Transfer of Learning theory is often used in education and business. It refers to someone's ability to take skills and knowledge learned in one area and successfully apply them to a completely different setting. It's what makes someone with math skills good at physics. It's the thought that if someone is a successful manager of a food processing plant, they will be successful in managing an automobile manufacturing plant. Transfer is why FBI recruiters look for someone with an accounting degree, expecting them to be good at solving problems. People with excellent transfer skills view their experiences as continuous training for the next task, whatever that may be.

Read 1 Samuel 17:32-37. I'm sure you are familiar with this story. But instead of looking at the epic battle between David and Goliath, let's look at David's mindset as he approached the fight. We all know, from a worldly standpoint, David was undersized and under-equipped to face the Philistine warrior. But David was not undertrained. David felt he was well trained because of his previous encounters with a lion and a bear. To steal a phrase from the movie, "Rudy," David had been ready for this his whole life.

As men of God, we are to approach unfamiliar settings with confidence because we understand God has been training us the whole time. It may be the next phase of life, a new career, or a call to vocational ministry. God has equipped us to transfer our knowledge and skills for whatever is next.

When God calls you to something new, don't make excuses and try to convince God that you're not ready. Respond with the attitude of "I'm ready. Let's do this!" David didn't see the size of the enemy. He saw the extent of his training. He knew God had delivered him from two extremely dangerous land animals, and immediately started strategizing how to defeat the giant.

God can use your past, even those experiences you had before you became a Christian, to prepare you for whatever is next. Were you addicted to drugs or alcohol? God can use you to minister to those addicted to pain killers. Are you a construction superintendent? God can use you to lead a mission trip building schools in Uganda. Are you a police officer? God can use you to train churches for active shooter situations.

Stop making excuses for what God has called you to do. He's been training you this whole time.

LEARNING FROM DAVID

1. Write your own example of transfer of learning not discussed in this devotional.

2. When was a time you realized God had already prepared you for the thing He called you to do?

3. You may not know what God has in store for you, but you can bet He's preparing you for it right now. What are you currently doing that God could potentially use down the road?

4. God has called you to use your gifts in some form of ministry. What barriers are keeping you from doing what God has called you to do?

5. What is your plan to overcome those barriers?

DAVID DAY 2

Have you ever had a loved one who was sick or in the hospital for any length of time? If so, then you know there are two types of people: those who tell you "let me know if you need anything," and those who show up at your door with a car full of groceries. There is a culture of "doing" and not just "saying" at my church. When my dad had a lung transplant in the summer of 2018, my family was overwhelmed at the response of those who provided meals, groceries, coffee, and even money without even being asked.

These people saw the need and chose to be the one to fill it. They didn't just talk a good game, they took care of business and even after they were done, they looked for more ways to help.

Read 1 Samuel 17:38-40. When David picked up five smooth stones from the river, he was doing more than stockpiling ammunition. I'm convinced he was preparing to fight the four other Philistine giants mentioned in 2 Samuel 21:15-22. You see, Goliath wasn't the only giant in Philistia. There were four others that we know of who were just as big or bigger than Goliath. David knew the Israelites would continually face opposition from the Philistines and he was just the man to defeat them. David refused to do just the bare minimum and call it a day. He was ready to go above and beyond the current battle. David knew God would give him victory over all five of these giants, but he was the one who had to pick up the stones.

Some men like to talk a good game and pretend like they want to be used by God, but when the opportunity arises, they are either nowhere to be seen or do the bare minimum just to say they helped. They do enough to check the box, and that's all. This is the man who likes to talk about helping others but never volunteers his time. This is the man who loves praying for missionaries at church but is too afraid to tell his coworker about Jesus. This is the man who says it's important to attend church but is at the lake every weekend. This is the man who likes to complain at the business meetings but doesn't tithe his money. There are two types of people in this world: talkers and doers. Let it be your goal to be a man who isn't just a talker, but instead is someone who picks up the stones and is ready for action.

Which one are you? I know the one every man aspires to be, but do you have evidence in your life to back it up? If God were to peek into your ammo pouch, what would he see?

LEARNING FROM DAVID

1. Think of a time you told someone, "Let me know if you need anything." Is there something you could've actually done to help that person instead of merely saying you'd be happy to help?

2. Circle the word that best describes what keeps you from putting actions to your words.
- Laziness
- Time
- Finances
- Apathy
- Image
- Reputation
- Envy
- Pride

3. Now, think of a way to overcome what you just circled. What scriptures remind you that God can overcome what you struggle with? Write it on a note card and put it in your bathroom mirror or use it as a bookmark to help you when you start making excuses for serving God.

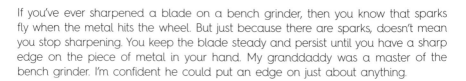

DAVID DAY 3

If you've ever sharpened a blade on a bench grinder, then you know that sparks fly when the metal hits the wheel. But just because there are sparks, doesn't mean you stop sharpening. You keep the blade steady and persist until you have a sharp edge on the piece of metal in your hand. My granddaddy was a master of the bench grinder. I'm confident he could put an edge on just about anything.

Proverbs 27:17 says, "Just as iron sharpens iron, so one man sharpens another." Men of God need other men in their life who sharpen them and who don't give up when sparks fly.

Read 2 Samuel 12:1-7. This passage takes place right after David slept with Bath-sheba and murdered her husband. Nathan was a prophet in Israel during this time, and God prompted him to confront David regarding his sin. When Nathan told David this parable of the sheep, David became furious that a man would do such a thing. He was irate! Then Nathan spoke the chilling words to him that cut him to the bone, "You are the man." It's a dramatic scene of David becoming painfully self-aware of his atrocious sins.

Do you have a Nathan in your life? Do you have a man who is close enough to you to call you out and stand by you when sparks fly? Men who are seeking to be the man God has called them to be surround themselves with men who love them too much to let them keep on sinning. Real love in a friendship is not accepting the other's sin. It's loving them enough to confront their sin with the spirit of grace and forgiveness.

Over the last decade, our culture has defined love as letting others wallow in their sin as we applaud them from the sidelines. That's not love. That's apathy. You cannot separate real love from the truth found in Jesus.

Think of your friends. Not your acquaintances, but your "I need a guy's night out" kind of friends. Your go-to men. Do these men love you enough to tell you that you're getting too close to the line with your coworker? Will they confront you about putting work ahead of family? Will they shoot straight with you if your casual drinking is becoming more than that? You don't need a bunch of "yes-men" around you who will cheer you on to your destruction. You need men who will speak truth in your life and who will still be around extending grace when the sparks settle.

There are plenty of men ready to point out your sin and see you fail. But it takes a real man of God to endure the sparks and stand by until there's a sharp edge on the blade.

LEARNING FROM DAVID

1. Write down the names of your go-to men, your inner circle of friends. There may be only two or three. There may be a handful. But most men won't have 10 or 12.

2. How would these men respond to you if you fell into a pattern of sin? Or maybe you have stories of how they DID respond when this happened to you.

3. Are you a Nathan for someone? Do you love these men listed enough to call them out and ask the hard questions?

4. How can you prepare yourself to be a better friend when they need a Nathan in their life?

DAVID DAY 4

SCRIPTURE PASSAGE: PSALM 51:7-12

Tray and Melody Lovvorn were married for eleven years when Tray's pornography and sexual addiction led to their divorce. In October 2008, after six years of divorce, they remarried each other with a renewed sense of restoration and commitment to Jesus and their marriage. This miraculous story was featured in the movie, *The Heart of a Man*. Now, Tray and Melody have devoted their lives to "Undone-Redone," the ministry of restoring marriages damaged by pornography and sex addiction. Tray is a man of God who didn't allow sin to win.

Read Psalm 51:7-12. David wrote Psalm 51 after Nathan confronted him about his sins with Bathsheba and her husband. David pleaded with God to renew him and create a clean heart within him. He was truly repentant. He fasted and lay face down on the floor for seven days mourning his sin and praying for mercy as his illegitimate son died. He knew he'd messed up and only God could restore him. From this point on, David lived with this dark cloud over his life. His life was anything but easy after this. However, he wrote many psalms of gratitude for God's mercy upon him. God was merciful to David and continued to use him for His glory.

Men, we are not immune to sin. Although true men of God establish clear boundaries and have safeguards in their life to protect against Satan's attacks, sometimes the temptation is too great to resist. A simple Google search for ministers with moral failures results in a heartbreaking list of men who were once regarded as godly but fell into temptation.

The saddest part is that many of these men never return to ministry. They never try to reconcile with their wife or family, and they view themselves as useless vessels. The devil laughs when we sin, but he rejoices when we render ourselves useless for God. When we stay defeated by our sin, sin wins. God is the God of restoration and love. Divorce does not win. Sin does not win. Defeat is not the end. Sin has been defeated, and God wins. Jesus has the victory over sin and for you to live defeated is to live outside of Jesus. Jesus, and only Jesus, allows us to have victory over sin—not just in death, but in life as well.

If you have messed up and think you are useless because of your sin, you're wrong. There's still work for you to do and the devil would love nothing more than for you to stay defeated. In Psalm 51:13, David realized he had more work to do. He says, "I will teach transgressors your ways and sinners will return to you." David saw an opportunity to serve and point others back to God as a result of being forgiven. God still had a plan for David despite his sin.

Remember, in Christ, we are not defeated by our sin, but are victorious over our sin through Jesus.

LEARNING FROM DAVID

1. What sin in your life has paralyzed you from doing God's work?

2. Why does God desire repentance when we fail?

3. What steps do you need to take to serve God after you've fallen into sin?

4. How can you help someone get their life on track after they've fallen into sin?

DAVID DAY 5

My dad was young and quickly climbing the corporate ladder within International Paper Company. When I was a kid, he traveled all over the U.S. and Canada overseeing shutdowns for different paper mills. One day he returned from a trip and watched from the driveway as my mom and I played catch in the backyard. As he sat in his truck, watching my mom do her best to stand in his place, he realized he had not been present in my life or my sister's for quite some time. He wanted that to change. So, he quit his lucrative role with International Paper and became a part-time mailman to be with his family more.

In February 2015, dad was diagnosed with Idiopathic Pulmonary Fibrosis, an aggressive lung disease that forced him into early retirement from the U.S. Postal Service. Shortly after, in a moment of reflection, he said to me, "I never told you the real reason I quit my job." I looked at him puzzled. He continued, "As I sat there in my truck that day, watching you play catch with your mom, it occurred to me that my son throws like a girl. It wasn't your mom's fault, she was doing the best she could without me, and you were just copying her."

Read 1 Kings 2:1-4. As David lay dying, he charged Solomon with these words. He blessed him and encouraged him. He challenged him to be obedient to the Lord, to be strong, to be kind, and affirmed him. I love the NIV's translation of this passage. Verse two says, "Be strong, act like a man." Solomon didn't have to ask what he meant by that. He knew how to be a man from his own father's example.

Sadly, so many children grow up without fathers, and young boys have no clue what it means to act like a man. Stats about the importance of children having a father's influence are too numerous to list in this devotional. But if a child grows up without a father, they are more likely to be incarcerated, get addicted to drugs, run away from home, or become a pregnant teenager.

A man who is striving to be the man God intends him to is a man who works to be a good dad. He isn't perfect, but he comes home after work and does his best to show the love of Christ to his family. These men put down their phones and turn off the TV. They are willing to give up financial security, recognition, and a great career to be present in the home if that's what it takes. They fight for their prestigious role as dads. They exalt in their children's successes and teach them through their failures.

If you aren't a part of your children's lives, what is your excuse? They need you. They want you. They might die without you. Don't get to the end of your life and wish you'd done things differently. Start being a man of God to your children today.

LEARNING FROM DAVID

1. Based on how you REALISTICALLY spend your time and energy, rank the following in order of importance by putting a 1-5 beside them (1 is most important).

Work ___
Church ___
Family ___
Social media ___
Hobbies ___

2. If I were to have your children fill this out for you, what would they say about you? Would their order be different than yours?

3. There are two types of values: aspirational and actual. Aspirational values are things you really wish were valuable, but your actions say otherwise. Actual values are the things you "actually" value based on your actions. Write an Aspirational value in your life. (For example, spending time with my kids.)

4. Now, look at how you spend your time and write what your actual values are.

5. What steps do you need to take to put your family at the top of your actual values?

WEEK 5:

ELIJAH

Stanislav Petrov.

Have you ever heard of him? Chances are that you haven't. And yet, if it weren't for him, you may very well not be reading this book.

Petrov was a Russian soldier during the height of the Cold War. He worked at one of the early warning facilities in the former U.S.S.R. where he was responsible for monitoring whether or not the U.S. had launched a nuclear attack on the Soviet Union. On September 26, 1983, the system he monitored began to report a nuclear launch against Russia by the U.S. In all, the system said that the U.S. had launched five nuclear missiles. Petrov was to notify his superiors so that the U.S.S.R. could launch a retaliatory attack on the U.S. before it was too late. There was only one problem: The U.S. had not launched an attack. It was a false alert.

One call from Petrov would have undoubtedly triggered World War III. The Soviets would have launched a counter-attack to an attack that never existed. The U.S. would have in turn launched their attack. A nuclear holocaust would have resulted. Who knows how many millions of people would have been impacted.

But Petrov didn't make the call. Something told him it was a false alarm. He kept silent and prevented a catastrophe of historic proportions. And chances are, you've never heard of him.

Isn't it remarkable how an important guy like Petrov can remain relatively unknown? This week, you're going to be studying the life of Elijah. I chose to tell the story of Petrov because I think he and Elijah play vital historical roles, and yet they both remain mostly unknown. Elijah isn't a guy that most men have spent time getting to know. And that's a shame because his life is powerfully instructive to Christian men.

This week, take the time to get to know this mighty prophet, arguably the most influential prophet in the Bible. Look for what his incredible life has to teach you about your faith. Listen to what God has to tell you as you encounter this hero of the faith, maybe for the first time.

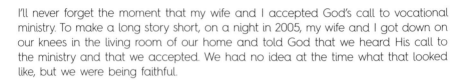

ELIJAH DAY 1

I'll never forget the moment that my wife and I accepted God's call to vocational ministry. To make a long story short, on a night in 2005, my wife and I got down on our knees in the living room of our home and told God that we heard His call to the ministry and that we accepted. We had no idea at the time what that looked like, but we were being faithful.

As I write this, it's been almost 15 years since we prayed that prayer, and I've been in full-time ministry ever since. I wish I had space to tell you all that God has allowed me to be a part of. And although I can look back and see where I could have been more faithful along the way, I know God has worked through me to accomplish His purposes.

Elijah bursts onto the scene in 1 Kings 17. (I'd encourage you to stop and read this chapter.) He does not appear in the biblical narrative before this moment, and even now we don't know much about him. But God had called him to confront King Ahab, and so he did. He told Ahab there would be a drought for three years, a sign of severe judgment. God told Elijah to flee to the wilderness where God would sustain him with water from a brook and food dropped by crows. When the water dried up, God sent Elijah to be taken care of by a widow. God miraculously provided food and water for Elijah, the widow, and the widow's son for the entirety of the drought. When the widow's son died of an illness, Elijah brought him back to life.

When Elijah prays to God and asks Him to heal the boy, and God listens and brings the boy back from death, the widow looks at Elijah and says, "Now I know that you are a man of God, and that the word of the LORD in your mouth is truth" (1 Kings 17:24). Because Elijah was faithful and obeyed God, he got to experience God at work.

When we allow God to use us as He sees fit, we get a front-row seat to watch Him work. Elijah knew this. He was faithful to God, and he got to experience God and God's plan in miraculous ways. Not only was God glorified and exalted, but Elijah was blessed. While not without significant challenges, his life was more abundant as a result. As a man of God, isn't this the kind of life you want? Don't you want to feel what it is to be utilized as a part of God's plan?

One of the powerful truths of our faith is that God chooses to work in and through us to accomplish His plan. God wants to use you. Are you willing to be used?

LEARNING FROM ELIJAH

1. In what ways has God uniquely positioned you to impact others with the truth of who God is and His plan to redeem all people from sin? How are you utilizing the position you're in to spread God's name far and wide?

2. We can be guilty of thinking that those who are vocational ministers are the "professionals" whom God uses the most or the most effectively. This isn't true. Maybe God is calling you to full- or part-time ministry as a career. Maybe He's not. But I can promise you this: if you have been saved by faith in Christ, God is counting on you. His plan to reach the world passes through you. Have you put yourself in a position to be used by God in your day-to-day life to bring others close to Him?

3. If you answered "no," if you look at your life and realize you aren't allowing God to use you, go to Him in prayer now. Confess your sins to God. Tell Him that you accept the fact that you are an essential part of His work in this world, and that you haven't been as faithful as you should be. Ask for the Holy Spirit to begin to shape your attitude and your will. EXPECT God to start to show you ways He wants to work through you.

4. If you answered "yes," begin to pray to God that He will show you particular ways He wants to use you. Ask Him to give you the awareness to see the tasks He has in store for you, and the strength to follow through.

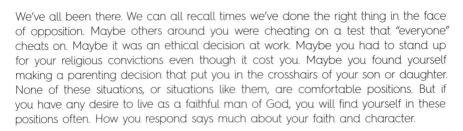

ELIJAH DAY 2

We've all been there. We can all recall times we've done the right thing in the face of opposition. Maybe others around you were cheating on a test that "everyone" cheats on. Maybe it was an ethical decision at work. Maybe you had to stand up for your religious convictions even though it cost you. Maybe you found yourself making a parenting decision that put you in the crosshairs of your son or daughter. None of these situations, or situations like them, are comfortable positions. But if you have any desire to live as a faithful man of God, you will find yourself in these positions often. How you respond says much about your faith and character.

In 1 Kings 18, Elijah found himself taking one heck of a stand. I want you to read the story, but first, we need a little background. Ahab was the king of the Northern Kingdom (Israel had split into two kingdoms after the death of David's son, Solomon). Like Solomon before him, Ahab's downfall was his marriage to a foreign woman who didn't share his faith in God. His wife, Jezebel, was a follower of the Phoenician fertility god, Baal (pronounced like a "bail" of hay). Ahab built Jezebel a temple to her god and allowed her to surround herself with false priests. With the queen as a proponent of this false god, Baal worship thrived, which was why God had sent the drought in the first place. As the drought reached the three-year mark, there was a showdown for the ages.

Now that you're caught up, read 1 Kings 18:20-40. This is a fantastic story, and to fully give it its due, we need more space than we have here. But let's focus on exactly what God did through Elijah. God was acting in a miraculous, supernatural way to show His people who truly reigned in Israel. Only God, the only true Creator, the all-powerful Alpha and Omega, could put on the kind of show the people saw that day. It was God's mic-drop moment to put the people, the false priests, and the corrupt leaders on notice. Can you imagine the scene?

God showed up big time. But let's not miss what Elijah did. Don't pass over the fact that Elijah confronted 450 hostile priests, a large portion of his people, and the queen herself. Talk about making a stand! Elijah's boldness is awe-inspiring. He allowed God to work through him in the middle of a culture that was almost wholly turned against God. On a stage that big, and amidst a group that hostile, Elijah could have shrunk from the moment. But he didn't. He trusted in God, and he did the right thing even though it was the unpopular thing. Because of this, God was glorified, and Elijah got to be a part of something amazing.

Don't you want to be the kind of man who trusts in God enough to take a stand no matter the consequences? I bet you do. Let's spend a few moments thinking about how we can go about accomplishing this.

LEARNING FROM ELIJAH

1. Make a list of the things that keep men from taking a stand for their faith.

2. Look back at your list. Do you see yourself in it? Of the things you listed, circle one or two that hit close to home for you.

3. Now, look at what you circled. Spend a moment and ask yourself if these concerns are worth forsaking God over. Yes, that's strong language. But when we shrink from boldly taking a stand for God, that's what we're doing. Is anything on the list you just made worth turning from God? If you can't immediately answer "no," spend some time in prayer asking God to help you examine your heart and your commitment to Him.

4. Jesus said in Matthew 5:11-12, "Blessed are you when others revile you and persecute you and utter all kinds of evil against you falsely on my account. Rejoice and be glad, for your reward is great in heaven, for so they persecuted the prophets who were before you." When it comes to standing up for God, it's clear: we should expect opposition. And we should still embrace the call to stand strong. Pray to God today asking Him to both show you opportunities to stand for Him and to give you strength when the moment arises.

ELIJAH DAY 3

Most of you reading this can recall a time in your life where you experienced a significant victory. I'm not talking about finding $20 in the pocket of an old pair of jeans (though that's awesome). I'm talking about a HUGE win. A State Championship in high school. Landing the big account at work. Shooting that trophy buck. Hopefully, you have experienced what it feels like to come out on top. It's a feeling that's hard to beat.

Elijah knew this feeling after his absolute beat-down of the false priests on Mt. Carmel in 1 Kings 18, which makes 1 Kings 19 so stunning. Stop and read 1 Kings 19:1-4. I don't know about you, but when I read this, it feels like driving a car into a brick wall. All the momentum from Elijah's victory screeches to a halt. After being a part of God's historic, miraculous win, Elijah finds himself in the pit of doubt and despair. What are we to make of this?

I think the takeaway for us is to remember that Elijah is human. Just like you. Just like me. While God worked through him in super ways, he was no superhero. Have you ever doubted yourself? Have you ever faltered in the face of adversity? I know I have. And if you can admit that you have too, then you know precisely what Elijah was dealing with. Sometimes, even in spite of all the evidence to the contrary, we allow ourselves to listen to those voices inside of us that say we're not good enough or that we don't have what it takes. Elijah certainly did. But let's look and see how God answered Him.

Read verses 5-8. In his brokenness, Elijah discovered that God had provided for him. God allowed him rest. God met Elijah's physical needs; He supernaturally provided food and water. God reminded Elijah of His presence; twice, an angel appeared to Elijah, even going so far as to physically touch him to dispel any notion that he was hallucinating or imagining it. And though we don't know exactly how it was communicated to him, God gave Elijah a purpose. He directed Elijah to travel to Mt. Horeb, the "mount of God," where God would orchestrate one of the most memorable moments in Scripture.

Elijah should not have despaired as he did. He should have been supported and sustained by the amazing victory God had allowed him to be a part of. But Elijah despaired anyway, and in his despair, we can see ourselves. With all that God has blessed us with, we have no logical reason to doubt and fear. And yet, we do, don't we? The most encouraging part of this story is that God didn't chastise Elijah. He didn't punish him. He didn't turn from him. On the contrary, God met Elijah in his discouragement, and He lifted him out of it. And the same God who lifted Elijah stands ready to lift you.

LEARNING FROM ELIJAH

1. Can you think of a time recently when you were discouraged or overwhelmed? Describe that time in the place below.

2. How did you get through it? Don't pass this question by. Stop and think about it. What did you do to get through your discouragement? List out your answer.

3. Now, look back at what you wrote. Where do you see God in your process of persevering? Did you turn to Him early on? Did you only seek God as a last resort? Or did you not reach out to God at all? What can you learn from how you sought God as a source of strength in a time of doubt?

4. God stands ready to meet you in your doubt and despair. This isn't theoretical. This isn't an empty religious platitude. God really and truly can lift you out of the dark moments of your life. You have only to turn to Him in faith. Remember this for when you need it, or if you need it today, turn to Him now in prayer, trusting that He is sufficient for all your needs.

ELIJAH DAY 4

Remember yesterday's devotion? Elijah had just had a great victory over the prophets of Baal. But one threatening message from Jezebel sent him running. Elijah fled to the wilderness where he asked God to take his life, a low point for Elijah, for sure. Recall that God sent an angel to nourish Elijah and to command Elijah to travel "40 days and 40 nights" to Mt. Horeb, the "mount of God." What Elijah couldn't have anticipated is what would happen once he got there.

Read 1 Kings 19:9-10. God finds Elijah in a cave and asks Elijah what he was doing in the cave. There is an implied rebuke that speaks to Elijah's purpose; God had called Elijah to be His voice to the people. By sitting in the cave, Elijah was taking himself out of the game. He was failing to fulfill his calling. His response to God revealed his frustration and despair. Elijah was having an old-fashioned pity party. But God wasn't having it. He commanded Elijah to go outside of the cave and stand before Him.

Now read verses 11-14. There is no surprise that God chose to reveal Himself to Elijah here. It was on this very mountain that He had revealed Himself to Moses as "I AM" thousands of years before. But what are we to make of HOW God revealed Himself to Elijah? God had revealed Himself to His people Israel through natural phenomena for ages. Pillars of fire. Burning bushes. Clouds of smoke. Storms, and so on. Elijah had just seen God envelop a water-soaked altar with fire from the heavens. Elijah wouldn't have balked at seeing God in the wind, or an earthquake, or fire. We can only guess, but it's safe to say that Elijah would have been surprised and amazed that God would show Himself in a "whisper." As miraculous as it would have been, God wasn't in the showy demonstrations of nature. He was instead in the personal, relational, grace-filled whisper that Elijah so badly needed at that moment.

When Elijah encountered the fire, and the wind, and the earthquake, it didn't stir him. But when He heard God's whisper, he rose, wrapped his face in his cloak lest he gaze on the holiness of God and die, and stood in God's presence. What a beautiful picture of a man who knows the voice of the One whom he serves! How fitting it is that God asked the same thing of Elijah, "Why are you here"? But instead of a gentle rebuke, this time the question held the tender encouragement of a God who was inclining Himself to care for the needs of His child. God encouraged Elijah, lifted his spirits, and gave him a new task.

God still does the same thing to us today. Make no mistake about it; the God who commands nature knows you and hears you. And the same God who controls the wind and shakes the mountains loves you so much that He makes Himself known to you and gives you life and a purpose. I don't know about you, but this is a God worth giving my life to.

LEARNING FROM ELIJAH

1. Are you guilty of putting God in a box? Do you miss God sometimes because you only expect Him to show Himself to you in certain ways? What can you do to become more open to who God is and how He may be wanting to reveal Himself to you?

2. Elijah felt like he was alone. God showed him that he wasn't. Not only was God present, but God reminded Elijah that there were hundreds of others just like him, serving God faithfully. What are the things in your life that bring you down and fool you into thinking that it's just you against the world?

3. Part of God how God lifted Elijah's spirits was to give him another task. God reminded Elijah that he was useful to Him. You are useful to God, as well. What is it that God has put in front of you that you are not doing? How would re-engaging with God's calling on your life help refuel your desire to be used by Him?

4. Spend some time in prayer today asking God to remind you of His presence today. Ask Him to reveal Himself to you in an unexpected way. Trust that He will do so.

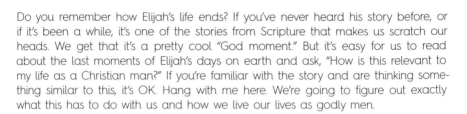

ELIJAH DAY 5

Do you remember how Elijah's life ends? If you've never heard his story before, or if it's been a while, it's one of the stories from Scripture that makes us scratch our heads. We get that it's a pretty cool "God moment." But it's easy for us to read about the last moments of Elijah's days on earth and ask, "How is this relevant to my life as a Christian man?" If you're familiar with the story and are thinking something similar to this, it's OK. Hang with me here. We're going to figure out exactly what this has to do with us and how we live our lives as godly men.

Whether you remember the story or not, read 2 Kings 2:1-12. What do we make of all the details? Let's start with the places mentioned. Scholars say that the locations Elijah and Elisha traveled to are significant. The locations mentioned here retrace the initial journey the Israelites made when they entered into the Promised Land. You may have thought of the parting of the Red Sea when Elijah parted the Jordan. That's intentional; it's likely why God had Elijah do this. It was God's way of bringing Moses to people's minds and establishing that Elijah was on equal footing with Moses in the course of Israel's history. There is also a repetitive exchange between Elijah and Elisha. What we're supposed to take away from this is that Elisha knew his mentor's life was coming to an end. He was heartbroken and didn't want to keep quiet. But he also wanted a special blessing from Elijah, signifying Elisha's desire to continue Elijah's ministry. But the real heart of the story is, of course, Elijah being taken to Heaven by chariots of fire.

From a theological standpoint, many scholars point to this as yet another way God was ironic. Baal was the supposed god of the storm. How fitting that once again the same God that brought down fire in front of the false prophets was ushering His prophet to Heaven in a storm of fire. God will not share His glory with anyone, especially with a false god who had corrupted His people's hearts.

God had the final word. His display of power at the end of Elijah's life was confirmation of the power He had displayed throughout Elijah's life. But this was as much a reward for Elijah as it was a moment for God to reveal His glory. Elijah had lived a faithful life amid constant opposition. He had wavered but never broken. He stayed true even though at times he was spiritually exhausted. And God, in His mercy, rewarded Elijah in a way that no one else has ever been awarded.

We have to remember that God sees us and knows us. He honors our faithfulness, always. While you may not be swept away in a chariot of fire, God is faithful and just and is quick to bless us according to His will. Like Elijah, we're called to be faithful and trust God to bring glory to Himself through our service.

LEARNING FROM ELIJAH

1. Can you point to a moment in your life where God seemed to bless or otherwise affirm your faithfulness? Describe the experience.

2. Why is it important to remind ourselves that God knows us and sees us? Why does this matter as we try to live our lives as godly men?

3. Elisha was persistent in his request for Elijah's blessing. Would you say that you are persistent in reaching out to God? Are you persistent in your prayers? Are you persistent in your praise? How do you think it would change your relationship with God if you could be more dedicated to how you communicate with Him?

4. Spend some time in prayer today surrendering your needs and wants to Him. Trust Him to answer your prayers according to His perfect will.

WEEK 6:

JOHN THE BAPTIST

Even though there is not a lot written about John the Baptist, there is still much to gain from what we have. His life and ministry served as the precursor to Jesus and is chock-full of takeaways for men trying to grow closer to Christ. This week is going to stretch you to be more introspective. The goal for this week is for you to look deep into your actions and examine your motives based on what we learn from John the Baptist.

First, let's get straight on our "John's." John is a common name in the New Testament. Our guy is John the Baptist. "The Baptist" wasn't his last name, nor was it his denomination. He was called this because people, Jesus included, identified him with his ministry of baptism. There are other John's in the Bible that you need to be able to differentiate. John, the disciple (or apostle) is the John who wrote the Gospel of John, 1, 2, and 3 John, and Revelation. This is the John described as the one whom Jesus loved. John the Baptist was not John the Apostle.

From a worldly standpoint, John was an outcast. He left home at some point in his life and lived in the wilderness until he appeared publicly to Israel. He wore a cloak made of camel hair and a leather belt around his waist and ate locusts and honey (Matt. 3:4). He preached about the coming Christ. He preached forgiveness of sins, and he baptized those who repented. His message was simple, and many people followed him.

I can't help but imagine John as a fullback in American football. He was a selfless role player and the one who prepared the way for the real star, Jesus. He never accepted any glory, though many people put him on a pedestal. He always pointed to Jesus. He knew his job and executed it well.

As men of God, our job is to point people to Jesus. John arguably did this as well as anyone in the Bible. What better person to learn from than the one who did it the best? Over the next five days, you'll be challenged to consider how your life points others to Christ. Let's get started.

JOHN THE BAPTIST DAY 1

Peyton and Eli Manning, Ken Griffey Jr., Prince Fielder, Richard Petty, Floyd Mayweather Jr., and Kobe Bryant: what do these men have in common? These men are some of the best in their respective fields, yes. But the common thread is that they all did more significant things than their dads. Each of these men followed in their dad's footsteps and excelled far beyond their father's accomplishments. As a son, I know the urge to be greater than my dad. However, now that I'm a dad, I want nothing more than for my son to be better than I ever was.

Read Luke 1:66-80. Zechariah was a priest who was described as "upright in the sight of God, observing all the Lord's commandments and regulations blamelessly." When Zechariah's priestly division was on duty, he was chosen to burn incense in the Temple. This was a great honor to a priest, and it would have only occurred a few times in a priest's life, if at all. While burning incense, an angel visited Zechariah and told him he was going to have a son and to name him John. Zechariah was not able to speak after his encounter with the angel until John was born. But when he was able to talk again, his first reaction was to praise God.

What do we know about Zechariah? We know that he was a godly man. He was an honored priest, and he was chosen for a special task. We know that he prayed for his son. He also knew that his son would do greater things than he ever did. We can look at John and know that Zechariah raised his son to become strong in spirit.

What can we learn from Zechariah? Zechariah shows us that God honors those who trust Him and follow His commands. As important as Zechariah was, he knew that his role as a father was more significant. Zechariah teaches us to be fathers who pray. Like Zechariah, we should pray so fervently for our children that all of heaven knows their names. A godly man prays for his children to be used by God more than he prays for his worldly success. And like Zechariah, it's our job as dads raise our children to be strong in spirit.

If you are a father, your most important work is to show Jesus to your children. I don't care if you are the president of your company or work 60 hours a week at a manufacturing plant; your children need you to be there for them to point them to Christ. They need your help to love Jesus more. Your goal should be to lead your child in such a way that propels them to a deeper relationship with Jesus than they could have without you.

LEARNING FROM JOHN THE BAPTIST

1. Did your father pray for you? If he did, how did he pray for you? If you don't know your father or know he didn't pray for you, how would you have wanted him to pray for you? What specifics would you want him to pray over your life?

2. What difference does it make in your child's life when you pray for them?

3. Circle the one you value more about your child:
   a. Athletic success or a love for Jesus
   b. College choice or desire to share Christ with the lost
   c. Viewing you as their hero or viewing Jesus as Lord
   d. Extracurricular involvement or church involvement

4. Those questions are designed to make you think about what you value. The answer should be pretty apparent in each one. But use this exercise as a way of guiding you to reflect on whether or not your actions and your child's activities align with the perceived value you indicated in each of these in this list.

JOHN THE BAPTIST DAY 2

SCRIPTURE PASSAGE: JOHN 1:19-23

Have you ever been mistaken for someone else? That can be dangerous, insulting, hilarious, and also flattering if it's someone you admire. When John the Baptist came on the scene, people thought he was Elijah, the Old Testament prophet.

Why was John the Baptist mistaken for Elijah? They lived 900 years apart, but when people saw John baptizing by the Jordan, they immediately thought he was the fabled Old Testament prophet (whom you've read about already in this book). Remember, Elijah never died. Instead, he was taken up to heaven in a chariot of fire; many people thought he would return to the place from where he ascended to heaven—along the Jordan River. Elijah's cloak was made of animal skins and part of his identity in the same way John was known for wearing animal skins. But above all of that, I think people identified John with the same zeal Elijah had for God.

Read John 1:19-23. John had the opportunity to claim he was someone famous. He could've exploited this mistaken identity for his gain. However, John's response to this temptation was to quote a passage from Isaiah 40:3, "I am the voice of one calling in the desert, 'Make straight the way of the Lord.'" John knew his purpose was not to gain influence, fame, power, praise, or followers. John understood his identity as someone who was born to point people to Jesus.

You and I are no different from John the Baptist. That's right. You read that correctly. Your role in this life is the same as that of John the Baptist: to point people to Jesus.

As men, we want to be admired. We want people to look up to us. We especially want our spouses and kids to look up to us. But isn't it more important for those around us to look up to Jesus rather than us? If my children look at me and only see a good man, I've failed. But if they look at me and see Jesus, I've done my job. Just as the moon reflects the sun, men are to be reflections of the Son of God. Real men of God understand their identity only in relation to Jesus. We are not the Messiah, but we know Him.

The Bible tells us in Matthew 5:16, "In the same way, let your light shine before others, so that they may see your good works and give glory to your Father who is in heaven." When you do good works, are you seeking praise? When you help a hungry man on the streets, do you have to tell others? Do you find yourself trying to take the perfect picture on a mission trip to post it on social media? What if nobody ever knew you did a good deed, would you still do it? When people see you, do they only see a good man, or do they see a reflection of Jesus—the perfect man? Real men of God would rather others see Jesus than themselves.

LEARNING FROM JOHN THE BAPTIST

1. If you had the power to change the way people view you, what would you change? Would it be a physical trait, or would it be something more spiritual or emotional?

2. Think of a time in your life where you nailed it, a time it all went really well. It could be the way you treated a stranger or how you showed your wife love or your child forgiveness. What did it feel like? Write it down in the space below.

3. When you get it right, when you do the right thing, do you think people see God in your life or do they see a better version of you? How can you ensure people praise God rather than you?

4. Pray that God will do two things in your life this week: show you opportunities for good deeds and for Him to get the glory when you do good.

SCRIPTURE PASSAGE: JOHN 1:24-28

Have you ever heard the phrase, "humble brag"? Even if you've never heard it, you probably can get the gist of what it means. For me, it's the guy in an interview who responds, "I would say my biggest weakness is that I work too hard." C'mon man. Nobody believes that. Humility is a missing characteristic in our world, and you seem to see it most in social media. Often people feel the need to justify their existence, and the result is outright bragging or portraying a false humility. Whatever happened to working hard and letting others do the bragging for you?

Read John 1:24-28. So many people followed John around; it was as if he was a rock star. In this passage, John was given the opportunity to puff himself up in front of the crowd but chose humility. Feet were nasty back then. Really nasty. Everyone walked on dirt roads where donkeys and other animals did their business right there in the streets. To touch someone's sandals meant you were a lowly servant. When John says he was unworthy to untie Jesus' sandals, he was describing himself as even lower than the lowest servant. How many people do you know as important as John the Baptist who would describe themselves this way and genuinely mean it?

Below is some of what the Bible says about humility:
- "Put on then, as God's chosen ones, holy and beloved, compassionate hearts, kindness, humility, meekness, and patience." - Colossians 3:12
- "Humble yourself before the Lord, and he will exalt you." - James 4:10
- "Let another praise you, and not your own mouth; a stranger, and not your own lips." - Proverbs 27:2
- "But he gives more grace. Therefore it says, 'God opposes the proud but gives grace to the humble.'"- James 4:6

Being humble is more than just being kind to those you supervise. It's more than rolling up your sleeves and taking out the trash in a company you own. It's a mindset where you see opportunities to elevate those around you rather than yourself. When you make your rounds to check on your employees, do they dread you or are you a bright spot in their day? Are they bracing for your criticism or are they anticipating an encouraging word?

Humility isn't what you do or how you do it; it is your attitude to others in response to your admiration of Jesus. Whether you are the CEO of a Fortune 500 company or an entry-level, part-time, temporary employee, you should strive for humility. Do the jobs nobody else wants to do. Avoid lording over those under your supervision. Strive each day to see those around you as people whom you can serve regardless of your position.

LEARNING FROM JOHN THE BAPTIST

1. Why is it so hard to be humble?

2. Write the definition of humility from two different perspectives:
   a. Worldly perspective
   b. Christian perspective

3. Think about the following areas in your life. Out beside each one, write one way you can practice humility this week:
   a. Family
   b. Work
   c. Church
   d. Other

4. What are some areas in your life where you need to be more humble? Ask God to reveal areas of your life where you struggle with pride and are boastful. Write them down and pray specifically for those right now.

SCRIPTURE PASSAGE: JOHN 3:27-30

The tradition of groomsmen in a wedding party has become skewed over time. Believe it or not, in centuries past, the role of groomsmen was much more digni- fied than a group of guys throwing a bachelor party and giving slurred toasts. Groomsmen, who were at one time referred to as Bride's Knights, were responsible for bringing the bride safely to the groom on the wedding day. They were body- guards for the bride and protected her until she was presented to the groom.

Although they were close to the bride, they were not the groom. When the cer- emony began, their role was complete, and they stepped back so the groom could receive his bride.

Read John 3:27-30. John saw his role as the same as a groomsman (the best man actually). His role was to bring the bride of Christ to Jesus. And this brought him joy! When John says, "He must increase, I must decrease," it meant that his job was complete and it was time to step aside so the groom, Jesus, could be the center of attention for His bride. From the beginning, John's role was to point people to Jesus: "prepare the way of the Lord" (John 1:23); "he is the one who comes after me" (John 1:27); "behold the lamb of God" (John 1:29). John knew his role in the larger picture of salvation. He joyfully stepped aside once Jesus came on the scene.

As men of God, what better image is there than to be bodyguards of Jesus' bride, the Church? We should assume this role with joy and revel in this honor. However, so many times we mess up our responsibility as protector of the bride. We fall short on our job because we forget that we are not the groom—Jesus is. When we put ourselves before Jesus, we find ourselves being selfish and passion-seeking. This behavior is sinful and has no place in the role of a man of God.

He must increase, I must decrease. As a man of God, I need to think less of myself and more of Jesus. I need to put less of me into my family and more of Jesus. I need to take a backseat and be joyful that Jesus is front and center. My career needs to be less about me and more about Jesus. My hobbies and interests need to be less self-fulfilling and more Christ-honoring. My relationships should be less about what I desire and more about how I can show Christ to the people in my life. My attitude in life should shift from what I can gain to how I can make much of Jesus.

As protectors of the Bride of Christ, the Bride's Knights, men of God should elevate Jesus above all else and be the chief servants to the Church.

LEARNING FROM JOHN THE BAPTIST

1. Why is it essential that we take on the attitude of John when he says, "He must increase, I must decrease?" What's at stake?

2. What is the danger in making more of yourself and less of Jesus in your areas of influence? Consider listing a few potential outcomes.

3. What is the benefit of making more of Jesus and less of yourself?

4. Think about a time in your life when you could've made more of Jesus than yourself, but you didn't. What would you do differently if a similar scenario arises?

5. Spend some time in prayer today asking that God would give you the wisdom to recognize areas in your life where you can decrease your influence and increase the influence of Christ.

If you have ever competed in an endurance race, you know the importance of training. There comes a time in every race where you hit a mental wall. You start to get tired and start to doubt your ability to finish. Your mind tells you to stop. You start questioning everything you think you know about yourself. It is at this point where you must keep pushing yourself. An often repeated saying in endurance sports is "Trust your training." When you've put in the hours on the trail, or your bike, or in the water, and you know what you are capable of, you can fall back on the confidence that comes from being prepared. This simple reminder helps so many athletes break through the mental wall in a race.

Read Matthew 11:1-6. This passage was at the end of John's life. He was weary, heavily burdened, and imprisoned. He sent some of his followers to deliver a message to Jesus. His question was simple, "Are you really the Messiah or should we look for another?" Jesus' response was very similar to Isaiah 35:4-6. Jesus' answer was threefold: first, he knew the reference to Isaiah would remind John of his training; second, Jesus reminded him of the miracles performed on earth; and third, Jesus knew John was about to die and was giving him a glimpse of what he was about to see in heaven. Each of these offered comfort to John in his time of doubt.

Should we be taken aback by John's doubt? Not at all. It's okay to grow weary when serving the Lord. We all have burdens in our life that get heavy. Going through seasons of doubt is okay. All this is completely okay, as long as you seek Jesus amid your doubt. When we seek Jesus in our times of doubt, He will reassure us of what the scriptures say, He will remind us what He has done here on earth, and He will reveal to us the promises of things yet to come.

When you are faced with trials and difficult times, doubt is a natural reaction. When a loved one dies, when you lose your job, when you have to file for bankruptcy and you lose your house, it's okay to doubt what God is doing. What is not okay is seeking answers to your doubt outside of Jesus. Jesus wants you to run to Him in the middle of your troubles. He doesn't want you to carry your burdens alone. Later in this same chapter, Matthew 11, Jesus tells us to come to Him with our burdens, and He will give us rest. Read Matthew 11:28-30 in light of the events regarding John that preceded it when you get a chance.

Seek Jesus and trust your training when you enter a season of doubt. Real men of God use their doubt as an opportunity to grow closer to God.

LEARNING FROM JOHN THE BAPTIST

1. When was a time you went through a season of doubt? What were some of the emotions you felt and the thoughts that you experienced?

2. What did you learn about God through that season?

3. How did God reassure you when you doubted Him?

4. When people around you go through a similar situation, how can you use your experience to help them seek Jesus?

WEEK 7:

PETER

If Peter were in the military, he would've been special ops. If he played American football, he would've been a linebacker. If he were a firefighter, he would've been the first one to rush into a burning building to save someone. I imagine him as a man's man who would have your back in a fight.

When we study Peter, it's like reading a tale of two men. There is the Peter we know before Pentecost and the one after he received the Holy Spirit at Pentecost. Peter before Pentecost was full of passion and zeal but never fully understood what it meant to follow Jesus. He was a "hit big or miss big" kind of guy. Before Pentecost, Peter walked on water but took his eyes off Jesus and nearly drowned. He claimed that Jesus was the Messiah but cut off a guard's ear. He boasted that he would never leave Jesus, but denied him three times. I could go on and on.

Many of us can relate to Peter before Pentecost. We see ourselves in him more easily as someone who knows a little bit about what God is doing and who Jesus is, but we don't fully get it right 100% of the time. However, we should strive to be like Peter after Pentecost.

After Peter received the Holy Spirit, he was a different man. While he never lost his passion and zeal, he became more focused and understood his mission. He preached with power and conviction, and he was instrumental in spreading the Gospel to people all around the region. Peter was thrown into prison, performed miracles, unashamedly proclaimed Jesus everywhere he went, and even died as a martyr. Because of Jesus and the presence of the Holy Spirit, Peter was a changed man.

As we look at Peter's life, let's try not to glorify the man we see before Pentecost—he meant well, but he didn't get it. Since you and I are on the other side of Pentecost, let's focus on how God used Peter through the power of the Holy Spirit being present in his life. Start thinking about how God can use you through the power of the Holy Spirit over the next week.

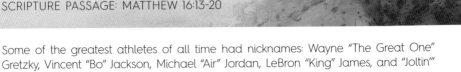

PETER DAY 1

Some of the greatest athletes of all time had nicknames: Wayne "The Great One" Gretzky, Vincent "Bo" Jackson, Michael "Air" Jordan, LeBron "King" James, and "Joltin'" Joe DiMaggio, to name a few. These men earned their nicknames based on their performance. Their nickname became synonymous with their athletic dominance. It became who they were, an integral part of their identity.

Read Matthew 16:13-20. Jesus was both trying to see what the crowds were saying about Him, but also what the disciples thought of Him. He asked them, "Who do people say I am," and Peter answered correctly. Peter said you are the Christ. Jesus' response was to call Peter, "Rock." That's an awesome nickname—Rock. Not "The Rock," but Rock. This name symbolized sturdiness. It spoke to the concepts of strength and steadiness. It was a name Peter could be proud of. However, remember this was pre-Pentecost and Peter was hit big or miss big. Just a few verses later, Jesus calls Peter by another name.

Read Matthew 16:21-23. Jesus called Peter a stumbling block, not a rock. He said Peter was tripping Him up. How does a rock become a stumbling block? By thinking about the things of man rather than the things of God.

As a Christian, are you a rock or a stumbling block? Are you focused on the things of God or the things of man? As those who have been saved by faith in Christ, we're men of God. It's time we act like it. Men of God look at things differently. They view life through a Christian worldview, looking at the world around them through the lens of the Bible. They lead people toward Jesus and do not trip others up by saying one thing and doing another. When they are attacked, they react with faith and humility. When a crisis arises, they see hope and not fear. When they discipline their children, they seek to disciple their child's heart not merely change their child's behavior. Men of God view their workplace as a place of ministry, not a place to succeed at all costs. They lead their family as an example of Christ to their wife and children rather than a man who worships work and self-gain.

Like Peter, we find ourselves living with the tension between our spirit and flesh. When our spirit is shining, we are a rock; but, when our flesh is winning, we will become stumbling blocks. The thing about stumbling blocks is that they affect those following us. It's our job as men to stay focused on the things of God and lead well. Be a rock, not a stumbling block.

LEARNING FROM PETER

1. Describe a time you realized you were a rock for your family, or in your workplace.

2. Now, describe a time when you realized you were a stumbling block for those following you.

3. Think a little more about the previous questions. What environmental factors affect your focus on God? Are their specific stressors that cause you to lose focus? Write down three or four factors in your life that cause you to become a stumbling block.

4. Now think about the other side of this question: what factors contribute to you being a rock? Is it when things are going well with your family and job? Or are you better and more connected to God in a crisis? Think about what makes you a rock and how can you more consistently be that man.

5. Spend some time in prayer today asking God to strengthen your resolve to be the man He has called you to be. Ask Him to remind you of the Spirit's power that is with you to lead you in godliness. Thank God for the influence He has seen fit to give you.

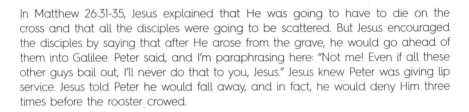

PETER DAY 2

In Matthew 26:31-35, Jesus explained that He was going to have to die on the cross and that all the disciples were going to be scattered. But Jesus encouraged the disciples by saying that after He arose from the grave, he would go ahead of them into Galilee. Peter said, and I'm paraphrasing here: "Not me! Even if all these other guys bail out, I'll never do that to you, Jesus." Jesus knew Peter was giving lip service. Jesus told Peter he would fall away, and in fact, he would deny Him three times before the rooster crowed.

Read Luke 22:54-62. Here we see Jesus' prediction coming true. In this passage, Peter denies Jesus three times. Verses 61 and 62 give me chills. Immediately after the rooster crowed, Jesus looked directly at Peter and Peter left the courtyard weeping. That is the last time we see Peter until the resurrection. Peter, Rock, the one who would never fall away, denied knowing Jesus three times.

Three days later, when the women went to anoint Jesus' body in the grave, they saw an angel who told them Jesus had risen. What the angel said next is subtle but powerful. He said, "Tell the disciples, and Peter, 'He is going ahead of you into Galilee.'" This is the same message Jesus said to Peter moments before the denial.

Can you imagine what it must've been like when these women burst through the doors and said, "Jesus is risen! We saw an angel, and he said to tell the disciples that he'd gone ahead of you into Galilee." I imagine Peter's head still hung low and ashamed for denying Jesus. Perhaps one of the women went over to him, knelt and whispered, "And he specifically said your name, Peter." Wow! What a picture of forgiveness!

John 21:17 tells us that several days after the resurrection, Jesus and Peter go for a walk along the beach. Jesus asked Peter, "Do you love me?" Peter said yes. Jesus said to feed His sheep. Jesus asked Peter two more times if he loved Him—three times total. Each time Peter said "yes," and each time Jesus said, "feed my sheep." It's no coincidence that Peter denied Jesus three times and Jesus asked him three times if he loved Him. Jesus showed Peter love by dying for his sins, forgiving him, and showing him compassion, not by just speaking empty words. Jesus wanted Peter to do the same and show Him he loved Him by his actions, not just his words. Jesus wants us to show our love for Him through our actions.

Godly men don't just talk the Christian talk; they live the life. God doesn't want fancy words and right answers; He can see through that. He wants you to show your love for Him through your actions to others.

LEARNING FROM PETER

1. The people who hurt us the most are the ones we're closest to. Think about some-one who has hurt you deeply. It may have been your wife, your child, your friend, or a co-worker. What made it hurt so much?

2. How should you respond when people you care about hurt you?
   a. When your child tells you they hate you:
   b. When your boss gives your promotion to someone else:
   c. When you don't feel that your wife respects you:
   d. When your friend goes behind your back:

3. Why is it so hard to forgive and show compassion?

4. When you think of the times you've hurt others and been disobedient to Jesus, does it make it easier to forgive others knowing how you've been forgiven?

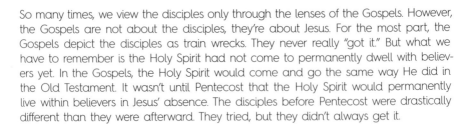

PETER DAY 3

So many times, we view the disciples only through the lenses of the Gospels. However, the Gospels are not about the disciples, they're about Jesus. For the most part, the Gospels depict the disciples as train wrecks. They never really "got it." But what we have to remember is the Holy Spirit had not come to permanently dwell with believers yet. In the Gospels, the Holy Spirit would come and go the same way He did in the Old Testament. It wasn't until Pentecost that the Holy Spirit would permanently live within believers in Jesus' absence. The disciples before Pentecost were drastically different than they were afterward. They tried, but they didn't always get it.

Look at Luke 22:56. Before Pentecost, Peter was a coward afraid to admit to a little girl that he was with Jesus. But later, we see Peter standing up for Jesus in the most public of ways. Read Acts 2:14-21. Here we see Peter as the apostles' spokesman to the masses. He boldly proclaimed Christ and would eventually die a martyr's death. The one thing in his life that transformed him from "coward to courageous" was the presence of the Holy Spirit.

The Holy Spirit affects every facet of a man's life. Who makes a hard man compassionate? The Holy Spirit. Who makes an abusive man kind? The Holy Spirit. Who gives an addict self-control? The Holy Spirit. The Holy Spirit turns a man's anger into love, fear to joy, angst to peace, restlessness to patience, harshness to kindness, evil to goodness, infidelity to faithfulness, gruffness to gentleness, and carelessness to self-control. Who can heal a marriage? Who can mend a relationship with a friend? The answer is the Holy Spirit.

What's more, your relationship to the Holy Spirit directly impacts your understanding of God's Word. And your understanding of God's Word is revealed through how you treat others. The Holy Spirit will never act outside of God's Word. He will always repeat and remind us of what God has revealed in His Word and done through His son, Jesus.

Peter couldn't transform himself into the man God made him at Pentecost; he needed the Holy Spirit. If you are trying to get your life on track and make significant changes in how you live, you will fail without the Holy Spirit. It is impossible for you to live a life devoted to Christ, to lead your family well, or to be a Christian influence in your workplace outside of the Holy Spirit. Additionally, if you are trying to live in the fullness of the Holy Spirit outside the Word of God, you will fail miserably. I'm not saying you need a seminary education to know God's Word—the disciples didn't have that. But you should be studying the Word regularly. God has given you the tools you need to understand His Word and the most important one is His Holy Spirit.

LEARNING FROM PETER

1. What does your time in God's Word look like? I'm not talking about reading books like this one. I'm talking about sitting down and opening yourself up to God's truth in the Bible. Describe your relationship to God's Word in a few words. Circle the one that best describes your Bible reading/study time.
    a. Once a day
    b. Once a week
    c. More than once a week
    d. Once a month
    e. I hardly ever read the Bible
    f. I never read the Bible unless I'm at church

2. Now, go back to question 1 and underline the phrase you'd like to see describe your relationship to God's Word.

3. What needs to change so you can get to the level you desire? What do you need to sacrifice to make this happen?

PETER DAY 4

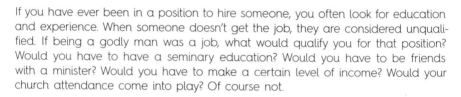

SCRIPTURE PASSAGE: ACTS 4:13

If you have ever been in a position to hire someone, you often look for education and experience. When someone doesn't get the job, they are considered unqualified. If being a godly man was a job, what would qualify you for that position? Would you have to have a seminary education? Would you have to be friends with a minister? Would you have to make a certain level of income? Would your church attendance come into play? Of course not.

Read Acts 4:13. The Sanhedrin were astonished by Peter and John's courage for preaching the Gospel and the miracles they performed. But it wasn't Peter and John's education or status that made them men of God. They were ordinary, blue-collar men. Both Peter and John were fishermen. Like many of us, they were familiar with hard work and long hours. They were not part of the upper class of society nor were they considered among the religious elite. However, what set them apart was that they had been with Jesus. Your occupation and education are not what qualifies you for service to God; it's your relationship to Jesus that matters.

I went to seminary, and I can attest that earning a Master of Divinity degree does not make you a better man of God. Don't get me wrong; the education gives you incredible tools to use for God's Kingdom. But seminary can be a spiritually dry season if you do not regularly spend time with Jesus outside of your coursework. The beauty of Christianity is that Jesus came to us so we can have access to Him regardless of our education or status. He allows us to enter into His presence through His Spirit and God's Word.

Like with Peter and John, the result of spending time with Jesus is service to others. If you are spending time with Jesus through His Word, you are fully equipped to lead and serve. Stop making excuses for not teaching that class, or leading that Bible study, or discipling that young man. Get involved! The devil will try to talk you out of serving others and make you feel unqualified. The devil will lie to you and say you aren't smart enough or important enough to serve. Don't listen to him. Nothing but your relationship with Jesus qualifies you to serve Him. If you are a Christian but are not spending time with Jesus through His Word, YOU are the only one keeping yourself from being used. You're on the right track by engaging in this book. Keep it up and get to work in your local church.

LEARNING FROM PETER

1. What excuses have you heard people using when trying to avoid serving in their church? If you're honest, how many of these have you ever used yourself?

2. Have you ever felt unqualified to serve in a leadership role in your church? What made you feel unqualified?

3. If you were applying for the job of "Man of God," what would qualify you for that position?

4. What area in your life have you felt God leading you to serve in but you have been running from?

5. Pray that God would remove any lies from Satan that would make you feel inadequate to serve in that capacity.

PETER DAY 5

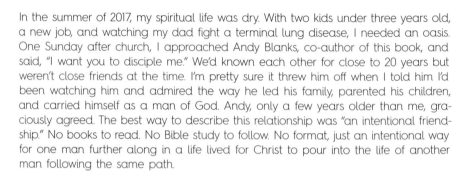

In the summer of 2017, my spiritual life was dry. With two kids under three years old, a new job, and watching my dad fight a terminal lung disease, I needed an oasis. One Sunday after church, I approached Andy Blanks, co-author of this book, and said, "I want you to disciple me." We'd known each other for close to 20 years but weren't close friends at the time. I'm pretty sure it threw him off when I told him I'd been watching him and admired the way he led his family, parented his children, and carried himself as a man of God. Andy, only a few years older than me, graciously agreed. The best way to describe this relationship was "an intentional friendship." No books to read. No Bible study to follow. No format, just an intentional way for one man further along in a life lived for Christ to pour into the life of another man following the same path.

Read 1 Peter 5:1-10. Peter believed in the power of mentorships. In this passage, he is speaking to two groups: elders and young men. He encouraged the elders to lead by example and the young men to follow with humility. I find it interesting that Peter tells the older men in the church to lead by example not out of obligation, but out of care for those under their watch. Just as compelling is his plea for young men to submit to the authority of those over them with humility.

To the older men reading this book, you have the responsibility to lead younger men. You have been given the gift of experience and wisdom that younger men need. Young men need older men to pour into their lives. You have so much to offer. It's your responsibility to help those following your footsteps avoid the pitfalls and snares into which you may or may not have fallen. You need to help the younger men identify the roaring lion on the prowl.

To the younger men reading this book, here's a newsflash, "You don't know everything!" (I know because I've been there.) Peter knew this all too well. He was young (and a little brash) before he received the Holy Spirit. Humility was not a word that would've been used to describe him before Pentecost. Isn't it beautiful how God took a know-it-all and turned him into a humble man whose life was spent in service to Jesus? One thing about Peter is he never lost his zeal, but he gained humility. As a young man, never lose your fire for life, but be sure you are humble even in your youth. Be humble and seek out someone to lead you.

If you are not mentoring someone, find a few men to pour your life into. If you are not being led, find someone to lead you. Don't be afraid to ask them to mentor you. I'm glad I wasn't.

LEARNING FROM PETER

1. Think of one man who has impacted your life positively for Jesus. What did that relationship look like? What made it impactful? What stage of life were you in when this person led you?

2. Think of one man you've mentored in an intentional friendship. How did you lead him? (If you cannot think of anyone, write down the name of a man you would like to lead. If you cannot think of a person, stop right now and pray for God to send someone to you.)

3. Circle the following excuse keeping you from leading someone.
   a. I don't feel adequate.
   b. I don't have the time.
   c. I don't know enough.
   d. Nobody would want to be led by me.
   e. I don't see my current excuse on here, but I have one.

4. Now, whichever one you chose, pray that God would take away these feelings. God wants to use you despite any excuse you give Him.

WEEK 8:
PAUL

The Apostle Paul is a fitting character with which to end this book. After all, we know Paul. You don't have to be a biblical scholar to have benefitted from his contribution to Scripture. Because Paul's contributions to the Bible are in the form of personal letters, we feel like we know Paul. We have a sense of his personality. We know a lot about his experiences. We know the kinds of things that set him off (I'm looking at you, Corinthian Church) and the things that warmed his heart. He had little patience for those who weren't sold out for the Gospel (see John Mark) but proved he was gracious and forgiving and willing to give people a second chance (see John Mark). Paul is a familiar character to us and represents a great way to wrap up this study of the men of the Bible.

Hopefully, over the next five days, you're going to get to know Paul a little better. But more importantly, you're going to have the chance to take Paul's life and measure your own next to it. You may find some areas that match up well. You may find others that do not. It's OK. Don't be discouraged. Let God begin to do the work in your life to shape you into someone fully committed to living out the Gospel. Someone like Paul.

I pray that this last week of devotions will remind you of the importance of completely giving all of yourself to be used for God's glory. As Paul shows us, there is no more fulfilling way to live.

(There's also a minor point I'd like to make here: I'm going to call Paul "Paul" throughout, even though he is referred to as Saul in the first two devotions you'll read. It's just easier that way. Also, this seems like a good place for me to climb up on my soapbox and remind us that Paul's name was never "changed" in the sense that some people make it out to be. Well after Paul's conversion, in Acts 13:9, it simply says, "Saul, who was also called Paul." From there on, Saul is referred to as Paul. The reason for this is simple: like many people in his day, Paul went by two names (especially Jews who had Roman citizenship as Paul did). Saul was the name he chose to go by earlier in his life to reflect his Jewish heritage. But Paul was the Roman "version" of the name. It's likely Paul chose to use it in his role as the missionary to the Gentiles.)

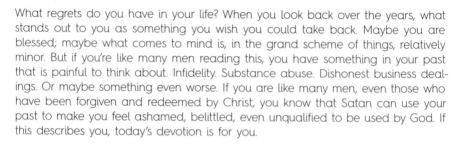

PAUL DAY I

What regrets do you have in your life? When you look back over the years, what stands out to you as something you wish you could take back. Maybe you are blessed; maybe what comes to mind is, in the grand scheme of things, relatively minor. But if you're like many men reading this, you have something in your past that is painful to think about. Infidelity. Substance abuse. Dishonest business dealings. Or maybe something even worse. If you are like many men, even those who have been forgiven and redeemed by Christ, you know that Satan can use your past to make you feel ashamed, belittled, even unqualified to be used by God. If this describes you, today's devotion is for you.

Take a moment and read Acts 8:1-3, but not before getting caught up on the context of the passage. The stage is Jerusalem. The atmosphere was charged. The Apostles were causing quite a stir with their preaching and their displays of Holy Spirit-empowered signs and wonders. Stephen, one of the leaders in the Jerusalem church, was making a significant impact. Described as a man of "good repute, full of the Spirit and of wisdom," Stephen enraged the religious establishment with his Gospel-centered preaching and teaching. They sought to seize Stephen, and inspired by the Spirit, Stephen gave an impassioned sermon lifting Jesus as the Son of God. The Jewish religious leaders couldn't handle it, and they murdered Stephen by throwing stones at him.

Look at Acts 8:1. Paul approved of this course of action. He was on board. And not just for the stoning of Stephen. Acts 8:3 says that Paul ravaged the church, going from house to house, arresting Christ-followers in the name of the Jewish religious establishment.

Do you think Paul, after all that he accomplished for Christ later in his life, ever had regrets about his role in persecuting Christians? 1 Corinthians 15:8-10 shows us that Paul did indeed feel regret for how he had acted. Regret is not an unhealthy feeling. It's reasonable to look back over our lives and to feel that we might do things differently if given a second chance. What isn't healthy as a Christian man is to feel shame over your past sins. When you came to saving faith in Jesus, your sins, your debts against God, were wiped away. Jesus purchased your innocence on the cross. If you have repented of your sins and have been saved by faith in Jesus, nothing in your past – nothing – can keep God from working through you to accomplish His purposes.

Take heart, brother. If God can work through the Apostle Paul, He can work through you.

LEARNING FROM PAUL

1. Why do you think Satan uses shame and guilt to make us feel unfit for God's use? Why are they such powerful tools?

2. What does it mean to you that God has freed you from the shame of your past? How does that truth empower you to freely serve God and to be used by Him to impact the world around you?

3. While God never leads us to sin, some of you reading this have a compelling story of God helping you overcome the effects of sin in your life. Is God calling you to use this story to reach others who may be struggling with similar issues that, with God's help, you have moved on from? Consider spending some time in prayer and reflection, asking God to show you how He can use your story to help others.

4. Do you have past regrets that you have not repented from? Maybe this is a good time to seek God's forgiveness and to consider any work you need to do to set things right.

PAUL DAY 2

I believe that God hard-wired us to love a good story. Especially a good redemption story. We're drawn to stories of people who overcome great odds to find purpose and meaning in the end. Whether it's a story of an athlete who overcomes personal hardship to return to peak performance or the story of how you faced down a pop-up thunderstorm and still managed to grill the perfect hamburger, we love a story with a good ending.

I'm not sure there is a better story in the Bible, outside of the story of Jesus Himself, than Paul's. When we think of who Paul was and who he went on to be, it's the kind of redemption story that never gets old. Today, you're going to spend a few minutes reading about the events surrounding Paul's reclamation. Stop and read the account in Acts 9:1-22, then we'll unpack it a bit.

First things first, it's a miraculous story, isn't it? Paul is headed to Damascus to do his thing when he very literally encounters the risen Christ. I have always thought it was funny how "high-and-mighty Paul" immediately knew his place; he was quick to add the "Lord" to his question of who he was talking to. He seemed to have an idea that he was encountering someone well above his paygrade. Imagine his shock when he discovered it was Jesus he was seeing. Talk about a wake-up call! I also want to point out God's interaction with Ananias. In this interaction, we learn something about what God intends for Paul. God told Ananias that Paul would be His "chosen instrument" to carry the Gospel to the Gentiles. I've said elsewhere that this is my favorite word-study in the New Testament. The original Greek means "the exact right tool for the job." God had a task in mind, an important one, and there was only one man for the job: Paul.

But let's pay special attention to verses 20-22. Look at Paul's immediate reaction once he was able to see. He did not wait to have an impact for Christ! He IMMEDIATELY began using his story to shine a spotlight on Jesus. People were understandably shocked. But it didn't stop Paul. I love vs. 22: "Saul increased all the more in strength." This isn't just talking about physical strength. It's talking about an increase in purpose, confidence, boldness, and influence. Paul wasn't satisfied with being "saved" and staying where he was. He sold-out to growing in his wisdom and understanding, and as a result, went on to become a powerful force for God's Kingdom.

What a story Paul's life is! What a fantastic journey he went on, from the chief enemy of the Church to an absolute powerhouse for God. As a man of God, there can be no more encouraging example of what is possible when we fully surrender ourselves to being used by God.

LEARNING FROM PAUL

1. What else jumps out at you from these verses? What stands out as significant in Paul's conversion account? Write your answers down below.

2. What do you remember about your conversion account? Maybe you were a child, and you don't remember much. Maybe it was recent, and the feelings are still hard to process. Take a moment and think about the feelings and thoughts associated with the moment you came to saving faith in Jesus.

3. Paul was God's chosen instrument to spread the Gospel to non-Jews. What has God chosen you to do? What task has He set before you? If you can't answer this, ask yourself: when was the last time you thought in these terms? When was the last time you asked God what task He had for you?

4. Spend some time in prayer today, asking God to show you precisely how and where He wants to use you. Then commit yourself to praying that God will give you the strength and the confidence to pursue the calling He's set before you.

PAUL DAY 3

It seems like it's in our nature as men to boast. As I write this, my son is about five years old. He routinely makes it a point to show me how strong he is. Out of nowhere, he will say, "Dad, watch this," which is immediately followed by him picking up an ottoman, or a gallon of milk, or the corner of our couch. I also have three daughters, each of them strong, each of them athletic. Not once do I remember them ever carrying on like this. There is something about how men are wired that makes even the youngest among us strut around like a peacock every once in a while.

In today's reading, Paul takes our natural tendency for boastfulness and flips it on its head. There was a vocal minority in the Corinthian church who were trying to undermine Paul's authority. So, Paul begins to list out all of the reasons why his ministry is valid. He admits that this boasting is foolish, but he is trying to silence his critics. Read 2 Corinthians 11:16-29. Here we see what the Gospel cost Paul. But instead of complaining, Paul lists out his trials as proof of his devotion to Christ. That's a great twist on how we tend to think about the tough times we encounter. But this isn't where I want to focus all of our attention.

Read 2 Corinthians 12:7-10. Here Paul acknowledges that he is the real deal and that there is very little room to attack the authenticity of his devotion to Christ. But he points to an unknown trial ("a thorn in the flesh") as God's way of keeping him humble. Now, people have speculated for centuries whether this was a physical ailment (such as chronic problems with his eyes) or a spiritual one (a temptation of some kind). But the nature of the "thorn" isn't as important as what Paul said about how he chose to process it.

Look at verse 9. God spoke to Paul and essentially told him that the purpose behind this trial was to teach him that it wasn't his ministry pedigree that empowered his effectiveness. It was the grace of God in Paul that drove him. God showed Paul that only through our weakness is God's power perfected, and Paul got it! So much so that Paul reframed what he would choose to boast about. Paul chose to boast not about his strength, but his weakness. Paul willingly set aside the confidence he had in himself and his abilities, realizing that the most effective way to impact the world around him for Christ was to completely rely on God alone.

God wants you to be a commanding presence at work in the world around you. But He wants you to do so out of a spirit of humility. The only thing we should boast about is how reliant we are on God. Grasp this concept, and you'll watch God use you in ways you may have never imagined.

LEARNING FROM PAUL

1. You may have been raised to be self-reliant. I was, and I work to instill this value in my children. When Paul speaks about boasting in our weakness, he is not talking about a lack of self-reliance or a lack of commitment. How do you interpret what Paul means when he says that he boasts "more gladly of my weaknesses, so that the power of Christ may rest upon me"?

2. What is the danger of us trying to rely on our talents and strength, and not the Lord working in and through us, to live our lives each day?

3. What is it about us as men that causes us to approach work (even Kingdom work) as something we have to accomplish with no help? What are some practical ways that you can begin to rely more on God's strength and less on your own?

4. Spend some time in prayer, asking God to begin to work in you to make you more reliant on Him. (This isn't a discipline that happens overnight; make it a point to pray this for the next few days, weeks, and months.)

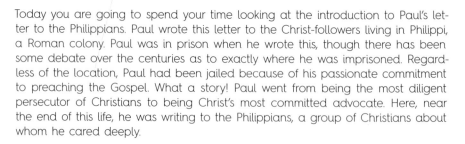

PAUL DAY 4

Today you are going to spend your time looking at the introduction to Paul's letter to the Philippians. Paul wrote this letter to the Christ-followers living in Philippi, a Roman colony. Paul was in prison when he wrote this, though there has been some debate over the centuries as to exactly where he was imprisoned. Regardless of the location, Paul had been jailed because of his passionate commitment to preaching the Gospel. What a story! Paul went from being the most diligent persecutor of Christians to being Christ's most committed advocate. Here, near the end of this life, he was writing to the Philippians, a group of Christians about whom he cared deeply.

Right out of the gate, Paul makes one of the most profound statements he would make in all of his letters. Paul catches the Philippians up on what's been going on in his life. He thanks them for their concern for him while he is imprisoned. He assures them that it's actually a good thing that he is imprisoned (talk about an unbelievable perspective!) because his imprisonment has served to spread the Gospel more effectively, even to his guards. But it's what Paul says in verses 15-21 that is so powerful.

Read Philippians 1:15-21. Paul starts by talking about how some people have used his imprisonment as a way of propping up their ministries and bringing his down. In a bold profession of grace, Paul says in verse 18 that he doesn't care what people say about him, only that the Gospel is advanced. What incredible humility from this man. Paul then says something that I want you to focus on today and in the days following.

Paul reminds the Philippians that even after being thrown in jail, he believes God will work to honor Himself through his life. Then Paul makes a profound statement. He says, in essence, that he believed God would indeed be glorified through his life because for him, "to live is Christ, and to die is gain."

Brother, is there a better goal to strive for? The aim of every Christian man should be to live in such a way that your very life could be described with one word: Jesus. Do your actions radiate the love of Jesus to those around you? Do your words echo God's words? Does a knowledge of God motivate your thoughts? If I asked your children or your spouse if they saw Jesus in you every day, how would they answer? What about your co-workers?

To truly live is to live as Christ would live if He were in your shoes, doing life in the context you do life in, day in, and day out. What is keeping you from living this kind of life?

LEARNING FROM PAUL

1. Let's have a moment of brutal honesty. Think about your character. What are the main things about your character that are the most un-Christlike?

2. Give this some thought: How are these aspects of your character negatively impacting your faith life? What do they cost you?

3. If these areas of your life were more in line with the character of Christ, how would your witness be different? How might others view you differently? How might God use you differently?

4. Now, I want you to ask yourself the question and to contemplate your answer: Why would I NOT do something about this? Why would I NOT do whatever it takes to bring my life more in line with the person and character of Jesus? Let the weight of that question rest on you for a bit.

5. Brother, hear me say this: God desires that you obey Him and that your life is an imitation of His. He has given you His Spirit to help you. I urge you to make it a priority to prayerfully do the work you need to do to get rid of the sin habits in your life that are keeping you from having the kind of Kingdom influence God desires for you to have. Spend some time in prayer today, allowing God to work on you and to show you how much He desires for you to follow Him more closely. Open yourself up to His leading.

PAUL DAY 5

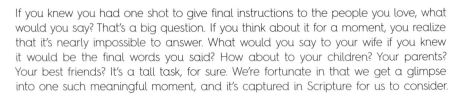

If you knew you had one shot to give final instructions to the people you love, what would you say? That's a big question. If you think about it for a moment, you realize that it's nearly impossible to answer. What would you say to your wife if you knew it would be the final words you said? How about to your children? Your parents? Your best friends? It's a tall task, for sure. We're fortunate in that we get a glimpse into one such meaningful moment, and it's captured in Scripture for us to consider.

2 Timothy was written while Paul while in his second imprisonment in Rome. He was in the last moments of his life. The Roman emperor Nero would soon martyr Paul in the ruler's infamous wave of Christian persecution. In what would be his last letter to his beloved protégé, Paul left some final words to Timothy that resound through the ages, and serve as a powerful reminder of how we measure our lives.

Read 2 Timothy 1:8-14. Here we see a man who is supremely confident in the life he has lived. Paul is looking back and considering the time on this earth he had been granted and whether or not he was a good steward of it. And we can see in his words that he knows he has done all he could do for God. He sees his suffering as a meaningful aspect of serving God. He sees the God-ordained work that God has allowed him to be a part of as a high and holy calling. He is not ashamed, not broken, not cowed. Paul can honestly say that He knows God, TRULY knows Him, and that this in-depth knowledge has produced nothing but confidence and assurance of God's presence and provision. And having considered the manner of life that he has lived, Paul can confidently say to Timothy, "live as I lived and you'll be alright."

Most of us won't have the luxury/curse of knowing when our last day on earth will be. But I have been around enough people as they breathed their last breath to know that the manner in which you live your life flavors the manner in which you leave it. The time to make sure you're making the most of the life God has given you is now, not later.

If every Christian man lived as Paul lived, wholly devoted to seeing the Gospel advanced, the world would look a lot different. But nothing is keeping you from viewing your life the way Paul viewed his. Nothing. The world needs men like you to surrender yourself fully to God's leading. What are you waiting for?

LEARNING FROM PAUL

1. Do you know God well enough to have the kind of confidence in Him that Paul had? If this were a season in your life where you committed to learning more about God, what would that look like practically?

2. How does your knowledge of God impact the way you live your life? How does it impact your decisions? How does it impact your attitude? How does it impact the way you see others?

3. Paul seems like a guy who was at peace at the end of his life. If your life ended today, would the relationships you leave behind be in good standing? Or would you leave some relationships in disrepair? Consider doing the work you need to do to, as far as it is up to you, repair any broken relationships in your life. You never know how God may work through your efforts at reconciliation.

CLOSING

We hope that this book has been worth the time you've invested in it. We can assure you that it was prayed over, both before and during its inception, and long after it was completed. We are guys who have both been shaped over the years by the influence of faithful men who have invested in our lives, some friends, some mentors. It's our prayer that our lives are shaping others as well, and not just other men. We take our roles as husbands and fathers seriously and strive to be men God approves of. We hope this comes through in the pages of this book, both in our words and in the examples of the real men we worked to highlight.

More than anything, it is our prayer that you embrace the call that God has put on your life to impact the world around you in His name. One of the most significant issues facing our culture, our churches, and our families are men who are not good stewards of their lives. They are complacent. They are apathetic. Or worse, they spend their lives pursuing things that don't matter. Our sincere hope would be that you are pouring yourself out to lead those people you have been given influence over closer to Christ.

What does that look like for you? We don't know. That's between you and God. But what we do know is this: God didn't save you to live a life of indifference. God called you to Him to powerfully work through you to radically change the world around you. If you hear us say anything, it's that the time is now. There's no more room to wait. The world needs you. God wants to use you. Don't do nothing. Do something. Get moving.

If we can help you in any way, please don't hesitate to let us hear from you. And if God has used this book to show you something new or insightful, we'd like to hear that too.

Thank you for allowing us to speak into your life.

God Bless,

Andy Blanks and Bryan Gill

BRYAN GILL

Bryan Gill has worked in higher education for the last 15 years as a college minister and currently as an administrator and instructor at Samford University in Birmingham, AL. After earning his Bachelor's degree from Auburn University, he attended Beeson Divinity School, where he received his Master of Divinity, and Gateway Seminary where he received his Doctor of Ministry. Bryan had many mentors along the way who helped him discover both his calling to higher education and his passion for writing, preaching, and teaching, gifts he frequently utilizes.

Bryan enjoys all things outdoors, especially fly fishing. He and his wife, Sarah, were married in 2006. They have one son, one daughter, and a yellow lab named Roscoe.

ANDY BLANKS

Andy Blanks is the Publisher and Co-Founder of YM360 and Iron Hill Press. A former Marine, he has worked in youth ministry, mostly in the field of publishing, for over 15 years. During that time, Andy has led the development of some of the most popular Bible study curriculum and discipleship resources in the country. He has authored numerous books, Bible studies, and articles, and regularly speaks at events and conferences, both for adults and teenagers. But Andy's passion is communicating the transforming truth of the God's Word, which he does in his local church on a weekly basis.

Andy and his wife, Brendt, were married in 2000. They have four children, three girls and one boy.

CHALLENGE A YOUNG MAN IN YOUR LIFE TO PURSUE CHRIST-LIKE MASCULINITY

Do you want to take your son, or a small-group of teenagers, through the same challenging content as you experienced in *How To Be A Man*? Now you can. The *How To Be A Man: Student Edition* follows the same daily devotions as the adult version, but it's written just for young people. It's a powerful way to walk with a younger man (or younger men) through the journey of becoming the man God has called him to be.

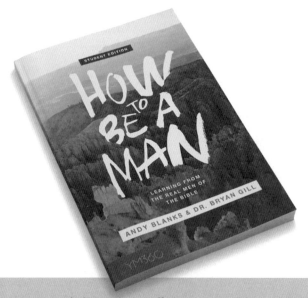

Because we want to help you be as effective as possible in walking young men through this book, we've provided you with a free study guide. We call it the "How To Be A Man Challenge."

TO ORDER YOUR STUDENT EDITION AND DOWNLOAD YOUR "HOW TO BE A MAN CHALLENGE," SIMPLY GO TO

HOWTOBEAMANCHALLENGE.COM

DOWNLOAD THE GUIDE FOR FATHER/SON, OR LEADER/TEENAGE SMALL GROUP. IT WILL EQUIP YOU TO OFFER AN EVEN GREATER CHALLENGE TO A YOUNG MAN TO IMPLEMENT WHAT HE'S LEARNING.

HOW DO YOU BECOME A MAN?
BY LIVING LIKE JESUS.

How To Be A Man: Pursuing Christ-centered Masculinity
is a 40-day devotional experience that will challenge you to a more passionate
pursuit of growing in to the man God is calling you to be.

Using 8 core characteristics, this devotional experience will challenge you to exemplify
these in your own life as you passionately pursue a Christ-centered manhood.

- Identity
- Integrity
- Purpose
- Surrender
- Passion
- Commitment
- Compassion
- Influence

SAMPLE IT ONLINE AT YM360.COM/HOWTOBEAMAN

IRON HILL

press

AN IMPRINT OF YM360

Iron Hill Press is a collective of people who love Jesus, love the Gospel, and love sharing those things with others through the medium of publishing. We've been serving youth ministry leaders all over the globe since 2010 through YM360. We're excited that Iron Hill brings to adults the same excellence in content and customer care established through YM360. Learn more about us at YM360.com or send us an email at hello@ironhillpress.com.

YM360.COM   ironhillpress.com   888.969.6360